I0414456

SHARED SACRIFICE

SHARED SACRIFICE

Don't Ask Don't Tell & The Global War On Terror

Gary S. Barkley

iUniverse, Inc.
New York Lincoln Shanghai

Shared Sacrifice

Don't Ask Don't Tell & The Global War On Terror

Copyright © 2008 by Gary S. Barkley

All rights reserved. No part of this book may be used or reproduced by any means, graphic, electronic, or mechanical, including photocopying, recording, taping or by any information storage retrieval system without the written permission of the publisher except in the case of brief quotations embodied in critical articles and reviews.

iUniverse books may be ordered through booksellers or by contacting:

iUniverse
2021 Pine Lake Road, Suite 100
Lincoln, NE 68512
www.iuniverse.com
1-800-Authors (1-800-288-4677)

Because of the dynamic nature of the Internet, any Web addresses or links contained in this book may have changed since publication and may no longer be valid.

The views expressed in this work are solely those of the author and do not necessarily reflect the views of the publisher, and the publisher hereby disclaims any responsibility for them.

ISBN: 978-0-595-48193-4 (pbk)
ISBN: 978-0-595-71847-4 (cloth)
ISBN: 978-0-595-60287-2 (ebk)

Printed in the United States of America

To all of the men and women who have served our country in uniform during times of peace and war. Their dedication and willing sacrifice for the people of the United States of America is both inspiring and essential to the preservation of our cherished liberties.

CONTENTS

Introduction

The war in Iraq, for me, is over. I now join the battle to retake my country. I opposed American involvement in Iraq before it began and I oppose it to this day. But I nonetheless am proud of having answered my country's call. I am *not* proud of what my country is doing here and abroad, but I am proud to have served. I am even more proud to have served with the officers, soldiers, sailors and airmen with whom I served. Every American in uniform should be proud of themselves, their service, their military branch, and above all their country.

You will read many times that this book is not about me. It is very important that I impress that upon the reader from the beginning. Let me say that again: *This book is not about me.* I am writing it to raise the alarm about the impending usurpation of our democracy by a corporate oligarchy. Some may criticize me for being too late, but where there is life there is hope—and the will and strength to fight.

This book will offend people, especially corrupt politicians, but I will not apologize. In this work I call 'em like I see 'em and I will not ask for forgiveness for speaking about the wrongs being committed in the name of the American people. For too long, political correctness has prevented many of us from calling a duck a duck. I will end my adherence to this rule now: I am tired of being nice. For decades the corrupt and incompetent politicians we have repeatedly elected to high office have betrayed us by starting unnecessary wars and mortgaging our future. But we can't blame only them: It would be unfair to hold only them accountable for the system we have let them set up in our name.

It is the nature of that system that creates an environment in which corruption and incompetence thrive and are rewarded. We have to recognize who is really in charge here, and who is ultimately responsible: We the People. We are to blame for the circumstances we now face and we are responsible for what will come from it. But with that responsibility comes the authority and power to change the situation.

In writing and publishing this book I am stepping into the public square, and I am fully aware and understand that I may personally become a target for derision by Right Wing chicken-hawks. These same people will undoubtedly call me unpatriotic for speaking against the United States government after I served in Iraq. I preemptively disagree. I find that my objection to the mismanagement of the Global War on Terror, and the limp resistance to it found in Congress, has given me the power of conviction to raise my voice in loyal and patriotic opposition.

Despite the fact that I have tried to make it clear that this book and its message are not about me, someone may try to "Swift Boat" me because they do not agree with the positions I take. Or perhaps there are some who served with me who disagree with the style of my service in Iraq, possibly because they didn't like some of the things that I said over there. Fine. I will accept their acrimony because I recognize that is the nature of discourse in this country today. In an effort to blunt possible hostility arising from the writing of this book, let me state plainly: I am not perfect. I have never claimed to be perfect and I know that I have faults—big ones; and selfishness does sometimes fall into my personal mix. But when the chips were down, when my country called, I went without question or hesitation and I did the duty I was assigned. Nothing more, nothing less. I don't believe there is a person who actually served with me in Iraq who could claim otherwise.

Throughout this book, I point out the vast profits being made by corporate profiteers. In the interests of full disclosure, I feel it is necessary to point out that I also personally financially benefited from the war. Due to my generous employer, who paid my full base salary while I was activated for the war, I was able to pay off all of my personal debts and come home to a tidy savings account. I only mention this preemptively. I have no doubt that the Right Wing supporters of the war, who also support the raping of our treasury in the name of no-bid contracts, would attack me for personally "profiting" from the war by accepting my wage. But I encourage the reader to remember that I *did not seek* deployment and I did not ask my employer for such generosity. I did the duty my country called me to do, nothing more. From a purely financial perspective, it was good for me. But the war has given me the conviction to speak against the wrongs my government is committing in my name. And that was a far greater benefit.

Because I accept responsibility for what I write, I naturally must accept any negative fallout from it. But I would like everyone reading this to remember that these are my words, not someone else's, and only I can and should be held to account for them. I mention this because I want my readers to remember that American servicemen and women went—and go—to Iraq, and not all of them go by choice. Whatever disrespect that you hold for our government (and it most certainly warrants a great deal of disrespect right now), please remember to keep your disrespect directed where it belongs: At the government.

There seems to be an intense anger over the war growing in American society. It is important that we do not let our anger and resentment of the policy boil over and scald the soldiers. I personally had such an incident in October 2007. I was riding home from work on the commuter train and talking with some co-workers. One of which has a brother on his third tour in Iraq. As our topic turned away from Iraq to shop talk, someone listening in on our conversation (it was a commuter train after all), confronted me stating that I should be ashamed about being someone who went to Iraq to destroy the country and kill the people. The person was so angry with me, that as he exited the train at his stop, he looked at me through the window and hit it with such force that the glass cracked.

The conversation that I was having with my friends was about what life was like in Iraq for the soldiers. We said nothing about fighting; we merely talked about the food and a soldier's daily life. The angry man on the train knew nothing of my opposition to the war or of my involuntary recall to active duty. He was simply angry at the war and took it out on a convenient target of opportunity: A veteran speaking in public about his war experience.

Once again, despite my opposition, I am very proud of having answered my country's call and gone to Iraq in the name of the American people. But I would like everyone who is also opposed to the war to remember the soldiers have nothing whatsoever to do with the policy itself. They are a tool of the government and the government is the responsibility of the American people. Take your anger out in letter writing, phone calls, protests—and at the polls—to hold your elected representatives at all levels accountable, but leave the returning soldiers alone (at least those who are pursuing private lives and minding their own business).

But in writing this book I am not minding my own business, I am minding the business of my government, which is my business but not solely my own: It is an important responsibility of every American to be involved in our self-governance. If we remain disengaged as we have proven to be over the past few decades, we will rightly see our free Republic replaced by tyranny. It *can* happen here.

While I have never had anyone explicitly tell me that being anti-war is unpatriotic, I have nonetheless heard the implication in their tone. Those that have taken this attitude are unfailingly people who have never worn a uniform of any kind. They wear the word "conservative" like a shield, hoping that no one will challenge them because they are conservative—as if that word alone should create unquestioning acceptance that the speaker is a brave defender of the Republic. Such bravado holds no influence with me. Let me make this clear: Bravery is actually putting your dick on the line, bravado is a swaggering coward with a codpiece.

While the main topic of this book is very serious, I hope to make the reader laugh at times. A combat zone isn't all-drudge-all-the-time. There were moments of levity in my Iraq tour. I like to laugh and I tried to keep those around me laughing as much as I could. I believe I succeeded and I want to carry some of that over into these pages. Enjoy.

Deployment

As I said in the introduction, this book is not about me and my main points are not about what I saw or did in Iraq. I'm writing about what I've seen and felt since I've been back. I have been told that since I am, nonetheless, a veteran of Iraq, people will want to read something about my experiences. So, I will devote this first chapter to my Mesopotamian misadventure.

Some people that were with me in Iraq might very well speak against me for writing this book, citing the fact that I did not come under direct enemy fire myself. Any modern army requires the work of support and "admin" personnel, such as I was, to make sure the paperwork gets done and that everyone has the resources they need to do their jobs. The time that administrative personnel put into doing their jobs often translates into rarely being able to leave the protection of the Forward Operating Base or "FOB", regardless of their desire to do so. I fell into that category.

Rush Limbaugh would probably call me a "phony soldier" because I didn't— and never have—supported the war in Iraq. It amazes and angers me to no end how someone such as Limbaugh (and he is certainly not alone) would use a boil on his ass to get out of military service during Vietnam and yet still be able to *sit on it* for 40 years straight (thank you, Mrs. Edwards, for making that point). And then he accuses those of us who actually *answered the call* of being phony. I do not believe it would be a stretch at all (or unwarranted) to examine his phony patriotism, but that would fill a whole other book.

It is true that, being an Operations officer, I fell into a daily office routine. But for those that have never experienced this, I want to impress upon you that it is important to remember that anyone placed in a combat zone for a prolonged period, whether they are regularly under direct fire or not, experiences the grind that comes from knowing of his or her constant danger, especially when mortar fire is coming in three times a week. That doesn't mean living in constant fear, it is just a grind. There is no simpler or more accurate way for me to describe it.

It is ironic (because that was the intent) that the radio call sign I was assigned in Iraq was "Rush". When I first received my radio, I was told to choose a call sign. I decided on "Grist Mill" (because that's how one officer in my barracks described my snoring). Everyone decided that the sound of that too closely resembled "Grizzly Bear" (at least over a radio), which was someone else's call sign. Because I am a vocal liberal—and proudly adopt the label—one senior officer thought it would be clever to call me "Rush", as in Limbaugh. So, for a full year in Iraq, when people thought of me, and needed my assistance they would call out the name "Rush". I'll never be the same.

Regardless of what Mr. Limbaugh and his ilk think of the actual soldiers serving in Iraq, we all had our assigned units and jobs. I admit that I got lucky in the assignments lottery, and I had a relatively easy tour. I am not ashamed of that. I would have done a harder or more dangerous job if I had been assigned one, but I wasn't—I did my assigned duty and left, just like everyone else. I also admit that I did not have the best attitude about serving in Iraq, but it is my observation that my attitude wasn't very different from that of others; I was just more vocal about it.

*   *   *   *

I was assigned to the Ninewa Provincial Reconstruction Team (PRT). I will try to limit my use of acronyms as much as possible, but I refer so much to this throughout this book that I will simply call it "PRT". During my tour with the PRT, I served under two colonels. I loved and respected both of them. But I couldn't help antagonizing the first one. He was a retiree who had spent virtually his entire career with the Rangers. If you have no Army experience, you can't understand the pride that these high-speed soldiers rightly have in themselves and their units. Needless to say, I was not high-speed, let alone a Ranger. But I simply could not resist giving this colonel a hard time. To begin with, I pronounced my rank like the British, "Leftenant", a habit I continued right through the tour, even after this colonel had returned home.

It is traditional—and required—that a subordinate officer salutes his superiors whenever he encounters them outdoors. But it often happens that officers who work constantly together will salute once a day and thereafter forego the formality. My colonel was a formal officer, but we both new of this custom, and one morning as I greeted him with my salute, I said, "Good morning, sir. We'll get that formality out of the way for the day." After he had given my orders for that day, he shook his head as he walked away from me. I shouted to him, "Sir, you might shake your head, but you *know* you love me."

In another instance, I was driving him and another officer to a meeting and as we passed a barber shop, the colonel noted that it was Thursday and he needed to get a haircut. I asked, "You get your hair cut every week?" He answered, "Sure, don't you?" I hesitated slightly, chortled and said, "No." At which time the officer in the back seat broke out in a deep belly laugh.

Like I said, I loved and respected this old man. And I know that he didn't like me due to my attitude, but he did admit to my commander that I worked hard and actually got stuff done. But he just didn't like me. He told his replacement as much. A few days before he redeployed home, he came into the office, looked at my commander, and asked, pointing to me, "Is his resignation paperwork in yet?"

The officer who replaced him was a National Guard colonel. I served most of my years in the military in the Utah Army National Guard. Two Guard guys tend to understand each other and can be honest with one another. One day, he came into my office and said, "Leftenant Barkley, I know that you were recalled involuntarily, that you hate the Army, and don't want to be here. But I respect that you came and are doing your duty. You work hard and do a good job. I don't agree with a word that you say, but I like you."

✳   ✳   ✳   ✳

You cannot truly understand my time in Iraq until you understand my training *before* Iraq, such as it was. I think the best way to sum that part up is: An enormous waste of time. How enormous? Let's just say that even the people *providing* the training admitted that. The following details may read somewhat like a travelogue, but I believe that it perfectly illustrates the absurdity of this conflict from the beginning to end of my *involuntary* Iraqi service.

My Iraq misadventure began on December 4, 2005, as I arrived at Ft. Jackson, South Carolina with about 100 other people. Each one of that group had been called out of the U.S. Army's Individual Ready Reserve, or "IRR" as we call it. Appropriately enough, we spent two weeks at Ft. Jackson learning how to be soldiers again: We were recertified in first aid, weapons firing, and Nuclear/Biological/Chemical training.

That first morning at Ft. Jackson, the Drill Sergeants (yes, they had Drill Sergeants in charge of us) tried to march us to breakfast. That was a sorry sight. A few of the older guys had limps, but tried to keep up. But even those without limps had a hard time staying in step during that short march. One Drill Sergeant said dryly (but correctly), "You guys are gonna have to work on that shit, you can't let soldiers see you march like that." They didn't try to march us in formation again after that.

Those first two weeks were fairly typical, if mundane. However, some of the things I will tell you regarding my pre-deployment training after those first few weeks are so outlandish that you, the reader, most likely will not believe them. Regardless, my experience with this training just reinforced the truth of a saying: "You can't *make* this shit up." In fact, there was so much unbelievable shit happening that we said that all the time! The whole deployment was a caricature. I kept thinking to myself: "Is this really how a modern military is supposed to function? I mean, you *just can't* make this shit up".

After our two weeks of in-processing and training at Ft. Jackson, we were loaded onto buses and sent to Ft. Bragg, North Carolina. We arrived at Ft. Bragg at about noon on December 17 and were greeted by a Master Sergeant who seemed genuinely angry with us for arriving by bus two hours earlier than he expected, on arrangements he was aware of that were coordinated between the staffs at Ft. Jackson and Ft. Bragg. What, scheduling mix-ups, in the Army? Who knew? Anyway, the Master Sergeant knew we were coming, he just didn't know what time—and arriving at noon threw off his lunch hour. Things steadily went downhill from there. I'm not kidding.

After venting his frustration at an interrupted lunch, the Master Sergeant greeted us, and told us, and I'm quoting here: "The living quarters suck, but at least nobody's shooting at you."

That was our welcome to Ft. Bragg. There I lived with my class for four and a half months in Building 5058 on the "Old Division" section of Ft. Bragg. These barracks were built for World War II, used for decades and later condemned. The Army needed a place to house all of the re-called IRR soldiers, so they *un-condemned* these buildings (without making any improvements) and housed us there. It is amusing to note that the chain-link fence that surrounded Old Division was topped with barbed wire, which was configured to *keep people in*, not out of, Old Division.

Calling our barracks "condemned" was too nice in my book. The officers were billeted on the upper floor of Building 5058 while the enlisted personnel were housed downstairs and in other buildings. The nightmare tour began with our latrine, which looked like something straight out of "Texas Chainsaw Massacre", right down to the hellish rust-covered walls and deeply cracked wooden roof support pillars.

The water in the building was not potable and there was no source of fresh water anywhere on Old Division—so we had to buy our own bottled water for drinking and brushing our teeth. No one warned us that the water was not potable, but it wasn't hard to determine that when it came out brown from sitting in the pipes overnight.

One officer described Old Division thus:

> *"It has been euphemistically described as "Splinter Village". It is the last group of the WWII-era buildings on Fort Bragg still in use. A funny way to describe: "These are the only buildings I have ever been in that should never be swept. The lead and other carcinogens (asbestos, etc) that are present in the airborne dust are more dangerous than living in the undisturbed filth".*
> *I have actually seen the Health Assessment teams on Ft. Bragg enter the same buildings we were living in while they were wearing full chemical protection equipment (mask, white suits, etc)."*

For our *training* and administration, we were assigned to a unit known as "Warrior Brigade". The name sounds appropriate enough, "Warrior Brigade." Like we've all just come back from a brief bit of leave and are ready to pick up the warrior mantle again. Hardly. I can already hear laughter at the mere mention of that name from anyone who has personal experience with Warrior Brigade. The laughter would be justifiable: "Warrior Brigade" *was* a laughing stock after all. Apparently the Army figured out just how big of a joke the name was. You see, we learned—after our return from Iraq—that the Army had taken things into hand and reformed Warrior Brigade while we were gone: Their exhaustive efforts resulted in the renaming of it to "First Training Brigade." Nothing else changed.

After a few days of in-processing with Warrior Brigade, the enlisted personnel packed themselves up again and moved to Ft. Dix, New Jersey for their pre-deployment Civil Affairs training. The officers remained at Ft. Bragg. Everyone was granted "exodus leave" to go home for Christmas. We had all just made tearful goodbye's with our families only three weeks before and we were sent back home for a two-week vacation, burning up leave time that we had not yet earned. At first, I thought this was a poorly-planned and organized operation, but I soon came to realize—along with everyone else going through this—that calling it poorly planned or organized was far too generous, because there was *no planning or organization involved at all*. I mean, at least poor planning would have meant that there was some actual *effort* at planning.

I don't know the details of the training that the enlisted personnel received at Ft. Dix, but upon return from Christmas leave, the officers went immediately to work training for our new jobs: Civil Affairs officers. We were height-weighted for record and took a Physical Training test (technically known as the Army Physical Fitness Test). You have to keep in mind that, with the exception of a few younger officers, most of us hadn't worked out in years and some were very over-weight. One officer, whom I came to like and respect, despite our polar differences in politics, had a calculated body-fat percentage equal to his age: 35.

Many people did not pass the physical fitness test, but that didn't matter. The Civil Affairs and Psychological Operations Command generally required anyone attending their Civil Affairs courses to pass the test before beginning the Civil Affairs training. But this was no ordinary Civil Affairs course, it was the "MCAC"—*Mobilization* Civil Affairs Course, so the rules didn't apply. I believe that this points directly to the poor planning of the entire war effort as a whole. It was obvious that they didn't have the troops necessary before undertaking this mission, yet the Administration chose to do so anyway. In order to fill out their ranks, they just changed the rules, and sent many who were not fit directly into a war-zone. With these kinds of requirements, maybe Rush Limbaugh should consider enlisting, given his high level of patriotism—heaven knows we need the troops.

Our class was made up of both Army and Navy officers. We spent three weeks in that course being trained by Civil Affairs officers who had experience in Iraq and Afghanistan. They did their best, cramming a normally months-long training program into a few weeks. It was designed to be a crash course to teach officers how to "Secure the Victory" through Civil Affairs.

We were taught some culturally important issues, but we did not get very much of that. The program was "death by PowerPoint", whereby endless hours of slideshows taught us our new duties. To be completely honest, the training turned out to be so irrelevant to what I actually ended up doing in Iraq, that I have forgotten for the most part even *what* they were trying to teach us in that course.

We had a capstone event in the form of a Field Training Exercise, intended to help us practice what we had learned in the classroom. We set up camp on a mock Forward Operating Base and executed missions by traveling to a nearby mock town built to represent a Third World village. The cadre of instructors would role-play with us to help us internalize our classroom training before deployment. In a lot of ways, that exercise *did* resemble a Civil Affairs deployment: Everybody was on the FOB at night and we ate whenever we wanted to.

After completing the Civil Affairs course, my class took a one-week course of instruction to certify us as "Combat Life Savers". That training demonstrated the latest in first-aid techniques developed using lessons from Iraq and Afghanistan. The major part of the course was spent on learning how to administer an IV to someone else. Interestingly, the Army has developed a self-applied tourniquet, in the happy event that you need to stop your *own* profuse bleeding and no one is around to help you.

✳   ✳   ✳   ✳

Many reserve units were scheduled to arrive at Ft. Bragg in February and March for deployment. Warrior Brigade had made some effort to assign IRR soldiers to these arriving units—which were undermanned from the beginning; no unit that deployed with us was fully staffed. People had to be reassigned quite a bit during the train-up period, and were "cross-leveled" from unit to unit in order to ensure that each and every unit met the minimum 80% staffing level. A unit could not deploy without meeting that minimum (waivers were always possible, of course).

Despite the state of manpower, Warrior Brigade was forced as a result of the Don't Ask Don't Tell policy to process out one soldier who claimed he was gay. The brigade was only a few weeks from deploying, and as understaffed as they were, they had to kick someone out for being gay. But you will hear much more about that policy in the next chapter.

Ft. Bragg's Old Division has many buildings identical to our Building 5058. By the middle of March, there were more than one thousand people—soldiers, sailors, and airmen—crammed into these dilapidated structures. It is no exaggeration to say it looked and felt like a slum. And these arrangements were made by Army leadership for Army personnel preparing for deployment to a combat zone—an inspiring tale of "taking care of soldiers".

Imagine the dim gray light of a rainy late afternoon, and further work your thoughts to see a lifeless and deserted World War II era Army post. That was Old Division. If you could *paint* depression, Old Division is what it would look like.

There were multiple complaints to congressmen about the conditions we were being forced to endure prior to deployment, but to my knowledge not one investigation was begun (even if one was started that I don't know about, the end result is the same: Nothing changed). Congressmen, who can always muster lofty words to show their unwavering support for the troops, would see no evil, hear no evil, and speak no evil in the conduct of this war, when oversight is their sworn duty.

One morning after breakfast, we were in a field being trained on hand-to-hand combat. It was a cold day—by Ft. Bragg standards—and the instructor didn't like it. He stated, "It's cold out here and I don't like being outside in the cold, so come back at 13:00 after lunch." A whole morning that could have been devoted to training was cancelled. I couldn't believe it: The U.S. Army cancels training due to being uncomfortable. Astonishing.

By the end of February, everyone in my barracks had been assigned to a unit, except me. But I was not the only person on Old Division unassigned. My "battle buddy" (my good friend and drinking buddy) told me, "We all hate you, but we secretly want to be you." He was referring to the fact that I had no unit and I had no one to report to during my weeks of idleness. My days were filled with pleasure reading in the barracks while everyone else was training. My buddy and I would go to dinner and have a few beers every night just to try to forget where we lived and what we were doing (or not doing, as the case may be).

Remember that wonderful planning and organization I had mentioned earlier? Well things were so well organized that the Warrior Brigade commander was forced to call a mass formation one morning to determine who was there and sort out the deployment personnel roster. Everyone went to the units that they had been assigned to for a roll call. I kept waiting, and waiting for them to call my name, but my name was never called.

You're not going to believe this, but things were so poorly planned and organized that it turned out that not only myself, but almost 100 others—nearly 10% of everyone in Warrior Brigade awaiting deployment—had *fallen off the Warrior Brigade roster*. You can't make this shit up! Once Warrior Brigade had discovered this grievous error, they created and assigned us to the new, "Battalion X".

The name, on its face, sounded exciting "Battalion X", like it was the secret tenth battalion, or maybe even a super elite squad of mutant soldiers, ala the "X-Men". The reality was far different. In all actuality, Battalion X was charged with making sure each of us "checked the boxes". Which is a perfect metaphor for what Battalion X stood for: We were reduced to putting checks, or "X's", in the appropriate boxes so that those in command could certify that we had been fully trained. You see, actually receiving valuable and useful training wasn't important, as long as everyone signed the training roster for each block of instruction. The quality and thoroughness of the training was irrelevant.

One morning, I was with Battalion X for some *actual* training on the SAW range (a SAW is Squad Automatic Weapon, a type of machine gun). The deployment Civil Affairs Brigade commander was there. He was trying to find people to fill his brigade staff, and what better place to start than with people who are unassigned? He asked me what "branch" (i.e. specialty) my military training was in—I told him Engineering—and what I did for a living out in the world—banking. Upon learning my skills, he asked me to join his staff as a budget officer. I agreed. However, I had to complete my pre-deployment training with Battalion X first. Additionally, I had to be formally assigned to the Brigade Headquarters in order to deploy with them.

I was excited by the possibility of something, anything, to do after my life in military limbo. With my new assignment already percolating in my mind, I went to Warrior Brigade to have the assignment formalized on the roster. To my surprise, *my name was not on their list.* I had fallen off again! Like I said, *you can't make this shit up.*

When I told the Operations Officer in charge of assignments that the Brigade Commander was requesting me for his staff, he told me that the Brigade Commander doesn't make those decisions and he would put me where I was most needed. It turned out that I was most needed in Charlie Company, 403rd Civil Affairs Battalion. I had an interview with my new Company Commander and he didn't know what to do with me (he later told me this fact as we were in Baghdad for the Surge), but he had me continue to finish my final pre-deployment training with Charlie Company. He ultimately had me permanently reassigned as the Executive Officer for Delta Company.

I will not bore you with the details of what a Company Executive Officer is supposed to do. At the PRT nothing was as it is supposed to be. Just know that I did whatever my unit and position required of me in the most efficient manner I could—and I received awards in recognition of that fact.

Delta Company was an administrative unit, not an actual formal company. I was informed of my new assignment late one morning during a training exercise. A major I had never met before called me to the side and introduced himself. He told me that he was my new Company Commander and I was his new Executive Officer. He also told me that we were going to Mosul, in Northern Iraq, to work on the PRT. I tried to correct him and tell him that the Brigade was still working on plans to send me to Baghdad with the Headquarters. He told me that I was coming with *him* and to "Pack your shit, bitch, you're goin' to Mosul". He left on the Advance Party three days later.

*   *   *   *

In late April, we were taken to the "Green Ramp" (that's the name given to the deployment departure/return point) to fly away to the desert. We got on the plane and it started rolling down the runway. As it was picking up speed, the pilot slammed on the brakes and brought us back to the terminal; there was a problem with one of the engines and he couldn't take off. After a few more hours at the Green Ramp, they bussed us back to Old Division for one more night in our old barracks—with no blankets or towels since everything had been packed for the flight.

The next day, we were in the air on our way to Kuwait. The flight stopped in Maine and Germany before landing in Kuwait some 20 hours after taking off from Pope Air Force Base (which is adjacent to Ft. Bragg). Charlie Company spent a day and a half in Kuwait before taking flight on a C-130 cargo plane to FOB Diamondback, located in Mosul, Iraq. After two nights there, we were split up into our teams—some of us went to the PRT on FOB Courage, others to outlying small camps scattered about the North, while still others remained on FOB Diamondback.

I arrived at FOB Courage via Stryker on Friday, April 28, 2006, along with several other new PRT members. Most PRT staff had arrived about a week before we did, so we were the final team members to get there. FOB Courage was located on the East side of the river in the northern part of Mosul. It was literally a compound of palaces on a hill overlooking the Tigris River. The 101st Airborne Division had taken the main palace as their headquarters and the Army Corps of Engineers had taken the only other intact palace as their headquarters. The largest palace on the hill had been bombed into ruins and was off limits for safety reasons.

The U.S. Department of State had set up a Regional Embassy Office on FOB Courage in the former residence of a high-ranking Iraqi officer. The PRT, being led by the State Department's Chief of Mission for the region, had taken the former houses of other high-ranking officers as office space for our various internal departments: Operations, Economics, Rule of Law, Governance, and Reconstruction. Aside from my duties as the military company's Executive Officer, I was also assigned as the PRT Operations Officer.

These two positions meshed seamlessly. In both of them, paperwork was my primary responsibility. This resulted in endless Groundhog Days. Let me tell you of a typical day for the Ops Officer/Civil Affairs Company Executive Officer for the Ninewa Provincial Reconstruction Team:

05:00 Wake up
06:00 Go to breakfast
08:00 Go into the office/Do paperwork
10:45 Go to lunch
13:00 Back to the office/More paperwork
17:00 Go to dinner
18:00 Spend the evening in room watching DVD's or surfing the net

See? Groundhog Day. It went on like that for months. Many people might say that doesn't sound so bad—but try it by force for a year. My buddy once put it like this, "Only inmates and terminal patients understand how we feel."

As I mentioned earlier, administrative personnel, such as I was, don't often get off the FOB (at least not routinely). Because we're doing the paperwork, getting the supplies, and making sure everyone else has what they need (their "beans and bullets"), so that they can focus on their duties: Winning the fight. For example, as the PRT Ops Officer, my duties required me to arrange air transport for our personnel when they needed to fly by helicopter or fixed-wing aircraft. I also coordinated security issues with the "Mayor Cell" (the FOB Commander's office). Despite the redundancy of my life on the FOB, there was one consequence of my captivity: I was able to observe more of what happened regarding contractors and their interactions with military personnel.

*   *   *   *

The day I arrived at FOB Courage, my commander took me around to show me how the PRT worked and what would be expected of me. He had experience with working on a PRT in Afghanistan and he told me that my main job would be to handle the contractors—the Bilingual/Bicultural Advisors (BBA's) and Local National Linguists (right or wrong, we just called them "Terps"). He did not exaggerate when he said that these duties would become my main focus. Managing BBA's and Terps takes a great deal of time. His intent was to give everyone a central point of contact for their administration, but more importantly, the unit needed someone to be "the asshole" when dealing with the contractors. That was me. I quickly came to understand what he meant by that standard and learned how to play the part. In fact, I received a medal for my efforts in this regard. Fortunately, the award citation did *not* read "For outstanding service as an asshole above and beyond the call of any other asshole". Instead the commendation recognized my efforts for "single handedly" setting up the BBA management program for the Ninewa PRT.

I had very little trouble with the local Terps. They were, for the most part, hard working and dedicated. There were some that didn't measure up to the advanced translation abilities required by the PRT and I had to let them go. But those that stayed with us through our tour were good people and I have a great deal of respect for them—they were brave to work with us and proved their loyalty to their country.

We had three very good local linguists (again, U.S. military personnel just referred to them as "Terps"). These three lived with us at the PRT most of the time, but would take a week off once in awhile to go see their families. We would arrange for their transportation if their families were in an outlying village. We considered them all to be essential to our efforts and every one of them was valuable, not just for their dedication, work ethic and skills, but also because they had become our friends.

One morning, one of these linguists came into my office to inform me that he was quitting. He had quit several times before due to pressure from his wife and daughters because of the danger his work was placing the family in, but he always came back for the good pay. This time, though, he said he would not be coming back. His son had received an ominous text message on his cell phone that said, "We know your father is still working for the Americans." This was a not-so-veiled threat, and the danger this created for his family was simply too great for him to continue to work for us any longer. He didn't return.

In October 2007, I received an e-mail from one of my former linguists. He told me that he had been the target of an assassination attempt over the summer of 2007 and had fled to Syria with his family, seeking asylum. He explained that Syria has very strict rules for refugees coming from Iraq and he had to settle his family temporarily in a village on the Iraqi side of the border. He remained in Damascus while trying to seek asylum from the U.S. embassy there. For his dedication to his country and providing vital services to American reconstruction efforts, he almost lost his life.

In contrast to the dedication that the local linguists showed, the Bilingual/Bicultural Advisors (BBA's) are another story entirely. That program is a true pork trough for profiteers. The concept of the program was great, but the execution of it did not match up with the idea. The idea was to take subject-matter experts in various fields, such as economics, law, governance, engineering, etc. and put them to work on the problems facing Iraqi reconstruction. The secondary idea—but nonetheless the one of overarching importance for the contractors—was that they should be from the West to teach Iraqi's how to do things the Western way. For some reason, we forgot the lessons of T.E. Lawrence, but the U.S. government was not about to let the lessons of history interfere with giving profit away.

T.E. Lawrence is best known as Lawrence of Arabia. He became the foremost Western expert on the Arab world of his time. His wisdom and knowledge of the Arab ways led him to conclude:

> *"Do not try to do too much with your own hands. Better the Arabs do it tolerably than that you do it perfectly ... Actually, also, under the very odd conditions of Arabia, your practical work will not be as good as, perhaps, you think it is."*[1]

This is a very important observation that Civil Affairs officers in Iraq ignore at their peril. Yet we were forced to use what resources we were given. And we were given mostly Westernized contractors to try to rebuild the Arab world in our image. It is a big mistake, and as should be obvious by now, ineffective and costly. It's not just costly in terms of dollars, but also time and most importantly, *lives*. Our methods prove that we are not, as a whole, trying to understand the culture that we invaded.

I want to give one example of the mindset of some Civil Affairs officers concerning this concept. One day, I was having lunch with several senior officers and one of them was complaining that the Iraqi people he was working with kept consulting with people he specifically didn't want them to associate with. His position was that we should just cut off ties with anyone that associates with those whom we consider to be bad elements. I countered his argument by noting that it is not our intent to stay in Iraq forever and who they choose to engage to solve their problems is more important, because they know the area and the culture better than we do—and they probably go to the right place to get what they need, our help notwithstanding. Thus we should encourage them to talk to whomever they need to in order to solve their problems—in essence we should *help* them take responsibility for the reconstruction of their own country, not dictate to them how it should be done.

*   *   *   *

During deployments, different units are on different rotation schedules, and they often overlap, so that you have to learn how to do business with someone new every few months in order to get what you need. Toward the end of my tour, a new BBA contract manager was named in Baghdad—the one who was there when I started had rotated out—and he came to Mosul for a first hand view of how our commendation-worthy "model" Ninewa PRT managed the BBA's. If you'll remember, or just in case you hadn't noticed by now, I'm very outspoken and don't hesitate to express my opinion when I believe I am correct. So, it should come as no surprise that during my conversation with this new BBA contract manager, I had a frank discussion with him about the program, despite his senior rank. I told him that I loved the concept, but hated its execution.

While the program sounded good in theory, and looked good on paper, there were still several fundamental flaws in execution. In my rather blunt fashion, I pointed out that our first mistake was not focusing more on how the Iraqi's traditionally do things. Secondly, my experience told me that we were hiring the wrong people for these positions. I concluded that the only way to make the program work would be to hire more *local* subject matter experts.

Throughout my tour I saw many instances where failure to hire locals was counterproductive to the BBA program's stated goals. As my conversation with the new contract manager progressed, I pointed out the example of one of our local Terps (the one who quit for safety reasons). He was an engineer who had been employed with the Mosul public works for decades before we invaded. Consequently, he knew everyone and was personally involved in most of the public works projects when they were initially built. My recommendation was that we fire our BBA's and hire, for much less money, locals to fill these positions. If we offered enough money—which would be substantially less than the Western-hired BBA's make—local professionals would flock to work with us.

By not hiring more local experts, we lost out on a vast wealth of institutional and local cultural knowledge that no amount of MBA's from Harvard could hope to replicate. Add to this the sizeable drain on America's coffers required to lure "Western" experts to Iraq, and the execution proves incompatible with the goals of actually reconstructing the country.

Before I left Mosul, I saw that the *idea* of focusing on local methods and hiring local subject matter experts had been substantially adopted in the plan for expansion of the PRT concept throughout Iraq. However, I don't know if these were actually implemented, but at least I saw them as part of a *plan* prior to shipping home.

∗   ∗   ∗   ∗

The Ninewa PRT was made up of Department of State, Department of Justice, Army and Navy personnel, along with USAID, and several private contracting companies. For the time we were on FOB Courage, and for a few weeks after moving to FOB Marez, we had Blackwater as Personal Security Detail for some PRT members going on missions off the FOB. Blackwater eventually moved to Baghdad. An Army platoon of Infantry and later Cavalry were assigned to provide the transportation and personal security to our teams. The military personnel were every bit as effective—and arguably more safety-minded in their planning—than Blackwater.

Being the Executive Officer of the military company supporting the PRT, it was my responsibility to lead the advance party to prepare our new home on FOB Marez. The PRT Deputy Chief of Mission, a colonel, joined me a few days later to throw his rank around as needed—and it was needed. We were a new unit, primarily Department of State in nature, despite being staffed overwhelmingly by military personnel, and the military-run FOB operations personnel didn't have a sense of urgency in providing necessary services. I'm not saying that they were completely uncooperative, but they just didn't see the need of going out of their way to help "The State Department" get the services we needed. The military "mayor" of the FOB, a lieutenant colonel gave us a great deal of support once my full colonel appeared.

On the move between FOB's, I had a great team of people working with me to set everything up and the night the main body of the PRT arrived, via Chinook helicopter, on June 1, we had their rooms ready and everyone went quickly to bed after a long night of waiting for the birds. After a few days, we had the new offices set up and the PRT resumed its work, with several missions a day going off the FOB to various venues around the city and the province.

It is important that you understand that a Provincial Reconstruction Team has no resources of its own with which to facilitate reconstruction. The PRT is a coordination center which tries to *convince* other units—and local government and businesses—to engage in certain activities. During my unit's tour, the Command's emphasis on the use and significance of these teams around Iraq increased dramatically and coordination meetings between military units and the PRT took on greater importance. The Ninewa PRT was considered the "model" of success for PRT's and was studied by the National Coordination Team in developing the implementation plan for the expansion of the concept throughout Iraq.

After the move to FOB Marez was complete, the Department of State Management officers, repeated in nearly identical fashion the mistake illustrated earlier by failing to hire a local engineer. They instead negotiated with a Turkish contractor the installation of high-speed internet and satellite TV into our housing units (we called them "CHU's", short for "Containerized Housing Units", which are cargo shipping containers configured for living quarters). They paid one-quarter of a million dollars *in cash* for the installation and a one-year service contract. He did a great job and we received the contracted-for installation and service. An essential part of reconstructing Iraq is to rebuild its economy, and that requires using Iraqi contractors as much as possible when doling out contracts. But remember that the engineer who installed our communications was a Turkish contractor, not an Iraqi, so the money he was paid never reached the Iraqi economy. The contractor took a vacation—and the cash—to Turkey when the work was complete.

The outsourcing of profit doesn't end with CHU's. Even though they are far from home, soldiers still like to buy things, so some units sponsor vendors to set up shops. Most of the vendors on the FOB are not Iraqis, they are Turks. The American military is averse to working too closely with Iraqis—at least when it comes to letting them set up permanent shops on the FOB—so the small trinket shops, barber shops, and tailors are mostly run by Turks. Service workers on the FOB—such as cooks and janitors—are overwhelmingly Filipino, hired by deceptive hiring practices. They are often required to pay a large fee to get a job—and become essentially indentured servants to the companies contracting with the U.S. government. One Civil Affairs officer cynically—and accurately—described the situation thus:

> "SERKA [a contracting company] *recruits almost all of their sanitation, food service, and facility support employees from the third world or from the lower classes of Turkey. Primarily, these workers pay a type of finder's fee of up to USD 1000. This fee is paid back from their paychecks once in country. And that country is Iraq. A country where unemployment runs near 80% in some regions to include Ninewa province. The typical SERKA worker has to work about 6 months before this fee is paid off. Unfortunately, in countries like the Philippines and Sri Lanka, this is a better option than being unemployed. Of course, none of these workers have medical insurance so too bad if your hand gets caught in the meat grinder, and they all work 14 hour days 7 days a week. We can only assume that the management at SERKA, smoking the happy hookah pipe and drinking*

chai [tea] *in Istanbul, is pleased with their contract with the U.S. forces. Turkey has long been a staunch ally of the U.S., and here again, we can only assume that this played a part in the Great Contract Giveaway of 2003 to present. Meanwhile, an Iraqi Shiite is being paid 50 bucks to blow himself up so his family of ten can buy a bag of flour."*

As you can see, it is not bad enough that these contractors are profiteering, but they are also employing essentially a slave labor force. This is strong evidence that the American government is trying to build an empire in the Middle East. But instead of using the mechanism of government as the dominant tool, corporations are now dominant in all areas, with the military now, more so than ever before, simply a government arm employed as a conduit of profit for private contractors. Instead of hiring Iraqis for a fair wage, and to give them a real stake in rebuilding their own country and economy simultaneously, we allow—and encourage—contractors to bring in an outside slave force to rebuild the empire to their own specifications.

✳   ✳   ✳   ✳

Shortly after we moved to FOB Marez, the BBA's had to go to Baghdad to have their identification badges renewed on Camp Liberty. My commander sent me along with them to observe the BBA-specific "badging" processes and learn the various methods for transportation around Baghdad. After the BBA's badges were complete, they returned to Mosul, I stayed in Baghdad for a short follow-on mission in the Green Zone.

My mission to the Green Zone was partly to assist in coordinating meetings between the Governor of Ninewa Province, an American general stationed in Mosul, and members of various Iraqi Ministries. In the end, there is not much two people, a lieutenant and a major, can do to coordinate such meetings in Baghdad. So, I spent four days at the embassy in the Green Zone, sleeping on a cot in a tent on embassy grounds with dozens of other "transients", and learning my way around that sprawling maze of a building. During my time there, I was able to get acquainted with the people running the National Coordination Team. These are the people in charge of coordinating all of the PRT's in Iraq. It was like a vacation. I spent the evenings by the pool with some friends I had made at Ft. Bragg, who were posted to the PRT in Baghdad. One of them even took me on a personal tour of the Green Zone to some of the monuments, such as the Iraqi

Tomb of the Unknowns and the military parade field with the crossed swords (which have since been torn down).

When I arrived back in Mosul, I settled in for a long, hot summer. My family had sent me a digital thermometer that I set up outside my CHU. It read 125 degrees every day. It did get hotter on some days, but the lowest daily high temperature reading until September was 125 degrees. We actually noticed it cool off when the temperature started topping out at 110 every day, and there was never a cloud in the sky. One night, we were expecting guests to arrive on a transport flight and I had to go pick them up at the air field. The flight was expected in the middle of the night and the thermometer read 102—at 2am! Ahh, summer in Iraq.

Pallets of water can be found almost everywhere, but they are in the sun all day, and most buildings keep refrigerators full of bottled water for anyone to take should they need one. Drinking water, like electricity, is never in short supply on a FOB (ordinary Iraqis are not so fortunate; potable water and electricity are in short supply throughout Iraq). One day in June, due to being so busy I found myself without water for about an hour. In 100+ degree weather, that's not good. When I finally had a chance to seek water, I found a 1.5 liter bottle and drank it in one draught. I didn't think it was possible to drink that much water without breathing, but I did it. I didn't even want air—I just wanted the water.

*   *   *   *

A PRT is a magnet for important personages. We had many high-ranking generals visit us, including the Chief of Staff of the Army, General Schoomaker, and the Chairman of the Joint Chiefs of Staff, General Pace. As a tradition, high ranking military officers give away coins to soldiers that they meet. The actual root of the tradition I have never learned, but the significance of these coins is that soldiers can prove that they have met, in person, someone of high rank. The practical aspect of them, so I am told, is that when at a formal event, the one with the highest-ranking coin doesn't have to pay for his drinks. I received coins from both General Schoomaker and General Pace.

When General Schoomaker visited the PRT, he was very generous with his time and offered to have his picture taken with anyone who wanted one. I gave my camera to a friend, and he being unfamiliar with it, took a few extra seconds to figure it out. During those few seconds, the general saw the Civil Affairs patch on my arm, and making small talk said, "Oh, Civil Affairs, where are you out of?"

I answered, "The IRR, sir."

He had retired once and was called back to take over as Chief of Staff, so he was also technically out of the IRR—and he said, "So am I."

My colonel, who was present, was also a retiree and chimed in, "Me too." So there we have it: An Army commanded and staffed by people who chose to get out, but were called back (although my colonel voluntarily jumped through many hoops to be allowed back in for his tour in Iraq).

An Army major told me a story from his time at Ft. Bragg that I believe would be an appropriate illustration of the Army's usage of the Inactive Reserve for deployments to Iraq. The major was walking with a large captain who had been recalled, just like so many others. The captain was breathless and sweating profusely, even though they were walking downhill. The captain said to the major, "Sir, I bet you think I'm a fat slob." The major replied that he didn't judge anyone; so many people had been called back from inactive lives and there was nothing wrong with being out of shape. The captain retorted, "Well, I am a fat slob. I was laying on the couch, literally with my hand in a bag of chips when the phone rang to call me back up. I told the guy on the other end that I was very overweight and I had no intention of getting in shape. He told me, 'Come on out, we'll find a uniform to fit you.'" *You can't make this shit up.*

The vast majority of the U.S. Army's reconstruction efforts fall upon the shoulders of Civil Affairs. Yes, the Corps of Engineers is there, but project assessments and contracting efforts are handled by Civil Affairs. And the bulk of Civil Affairs soldiers, at least during my time in Iraq, were from the Inactive Reserve. One of the Army's stated priorities is rebuilding the country, and this effort is handled overwhelmingly by soldiers forced into a job for which they have very little training, and what training is provided is "from a fire hose" (meaning that a great deal of information is provided in a very short time).

＊　　　＊　　　＊　　　＊

I went to Italy for my two-week mid-tour leave in November. When I returned to Mosul, I found it had greened up a bit. There had been some rain while I was gone and large areas that had been only dirt for my whole time there had sprung to life. The winter was mild, and it didn't rain as much as it usually does (so one of the locals told me), but when it did rain, the mud was a slimy ooze that got into and covered everything.

As the year dragged on, one day blending into the next, Iraq became one long Groundhog Day for everyone. Each PRT section had their missions to run and reports to write, while the Operations section did the same routine day in and day out: Ensured maintenance on the vehicles, made flight arrangements for those flying to various locations around Iraq, and feeding the parakeets (we had a large cage full of parakeets in the PRT's lobby). When visitors would come to the PRT, some would jokingly ask if we were using the parakeets as an early warning system for gas attacks.

*   *   *   *

As I have said before, I learned to have a great deal of respect for our local interpreters, but I gained nothing but disdain for our Western-hired BBA's. The sense of entitlement that these contracting profiteers had was grating. And I wasn't the only person angered by this. One day, a BBA who was transferring between one unit and another, stayed with us for what we thought was going to be only a few days. It turns out that our living accommodations were far better than he was going to get at his new unit, so he decided to delay his departure until my commander forced the issue. It was coincidence that we had scheduled a mission to the city where he was assigned and we put him on that mission for transportation. The morning of the mission, my commander asked him how he was getting from our venue to his unit, he said he hadn't made any arrangements for that. He expected us to do everything for him and if it didn't get done, "Inshala" (it means "God's will", in Arabic).

My commander flew off the handle at this unsafe view of the world and informed him that it is his responsibility to handle his transportation arrangements and, with a great deal of understandable (from my perspective) cultural insensitivity, shouted "Inshala is over!" Before you condemn this cultural insensitivity, you must keep in mind that the object of his anger is an American citizen of Iraqi extraction who has lived in the U.S. for over a decade, fleeing from Saddam Hussein's Iraq and when he returns to the country of his birth, he does it for *money*. I think insensitivity to this kind of person is appropriate. No BBA that I worked with had made any commitment to move back to Iraq—they were only there as profiteers (oh, I'm sorry, "contractors"), complaining about the size of their mortgages back in the States.

I had one BBA come into my office one day and complain that he had to stand in line with "the villagers", as he called the locals, at the dining facility. He objected to being subjected to screening by the Military Police at the entrance. He wanted me to do something about it so that he wouldn't be subject to the indignity of having to stand in line to eat. I told him that the security situation on the FOB is rightly handled by the MP's and I had no authority or desire to question their methods. He was incredulous at this and told me, "I am a member of Coalition Forces and should not be treated like this." To which I angrily corrected him: "You are *not* a member of Coalition Forces, you are a contractor. Coalition Forces wear uniforms and carry weapons. You have no more rights than I have, and I have to stand in line like everybody else, so get used to it."

We had one U.S.-hired interpreter believe that because she was a U.S. citizen she had the right to do with government property as she liked. We had satellite TV provided by the State Department in our CHU's. But this wasn't good enough for her; she wanted her *own* satellite system hooked up. So she started drilling holes in the side of her CHU for the cables. When I confronted her about it, her answer was that it was her right to do this because she had been in Iraq for a year and a half. This sense of entitlement was prevalent with all of the specialized U.S.-hires. It created more than slight resentment amongst the military personnel.

BBA's and U.S.-hired interpreters were not the only profiteers we dealt with, however. There were other companies contracting with the U.S. government to provide reconstruction consulting. It is interesting to note that it is quite prevalent that former American military officers (more than a few Civil Affairs officers) leave the military for the much higher pay that can be found in private contracting in Iraq. We had one former Civil Affairs lieutenant colonel who had served in Northern Iraq for his tour in 2003 come back for a slice of the profit pie. Some people would take exception to the use of the term profiteers that I use throughout my book, but I don't care. I just call 'em like I see 'em. One of the KBR Team Leads—the manager of the team that did the Operations and Maintenance on the PRT facilities—even embraced, albeit jokingly, "Profiteer" as his radio handle. As much disdain as I have for KBR as a company, their employees were outstanding.

Private U.S. companies, working for vast profits are not the only source of malfeasance in Iraq. Here is a story conveyed to me by a pay-agent Civil Affairs officer about how the Army deals with over-payments to local or third-country contractors:

> *"The contractor was paid for a service which everyone agreed after seeing the finished product was absolute crap. However, since a contract was signed, we, meaning the Civil Affairs money laundering company, were obligated to pay the contractor.*
>
> *I inherited this wonderful contract along with its $75,000 bill which was paid. This is where it gets tricky. The contract unbeknownst to me was reduced by $35,000. Of course, Mohammed the contractor didn't say anything. I think*

he bought a 7-11 franchise in Damascus with the overpayment.

While trying to clear Finance, I was told about this slight oversight. Of course, I shit a brick. But I didn't shit on the floor. I did want to maintain some pride. Anyway, I was forthright in revealing my oversight to Division Finance. Luckily, 40K is the equivalent to the price for a bag of Doritos in the Big Picture of financial folly that is OIF [Operation Iraqi Freedom]. *So I drew more money to cover the shortage and Finance made it balance.*

Here's a nice tidbit. Finance actually has a manual about using money in Theater. It's called MAWS or Money As a Weapon System[2]. And we know more people in Iraq are dying because of money as opposed to bullets."

Note that statement: "… Finance made it balance". He drew *more* money for the overage, *gave it back*, and that one transaction somehow balances the books[3]. He could only conclude that it was "Un-fucking-believable". But it is the only way that things like this can be done—the soldiers should not be held accountable for the dishonesty of greedy and untrustworthy contractors. This is just one example of how the Pentagon is the most unwieldy, wasteful and unaccountable bureaucracy in our government. *Even the accountants are unaccountable.*

✳   ✳   ✳   ✳

In December 2006, Donald Rumsfeld made a victory lap around Iraq before he left office in disgrace. He stopped, unannounced to visit the troops, in Mosul. As usual, I got out of bed early that morning and read the newspapers online (remember, I had high-speed internet in my room). One of the papers reported on a speech that Mr. Rumsfeld had given in Baghdad during this final tour. I read the transcript of the speech and moved on to other stories. When I went into the office that morning, I was told that we were all going to go to the theatre to see a special visitor—we didn't know who it was until we got there.

When Mr. Rumsfeld started speaking, I realized that he was giving the same stump speech I had read in the paper a few hours before. That's when I formulated a question in my mind. After he had completed his prepared remarks, he offered the floor up to questions. I had a good one.

Everyone who served with me knows that I am not one to keep my opinion to myself. As I had noted before, my attitude about the war wasn't necessarily a minority view, I was just more vocal about my views than others. So, as I'm sure you can imagine, when I was handed the microphone, my commander, who was sitting in front of me, turned around and said, "You be a gentleman or I'll kill you." I was a gentleman. Here is the text of my question as I remember it (I have no electronic recording):

> *Sir, Lieutenant Gary Barkley, 403rd CA, Civil Affairs I should say. During your speech you mentioned that you had spoken with a person in the hospital who stated that Americans just needed to show patience in order to see the strategy work. My question to you is: How can you justify asking the American people, and indeed us, to show patience for your strategy when you refused to show patience to weapons inspectors before the war?*

One officer from my unit later told me that he could hear the air being sucked out of the room from the collective gasp. There were several media outlets there, complete with large cameras (I have been told that the question was shown on Fox News and later posted on YouTube, although I didn't see it myself). When the tenor of my question became apparent, a camera a few rows in front of me swung around to get a view of my face. The people sitting around me instinctively crouched in their seats—one even made sure to cover the nametape on his uniform with his hand (after that question he said that I was a marked man and he would never travel in the same vehicle with me again—and he didn't).

I admit that my question was poorly worded in one regard: I made it personal—I said "... *you* refused to show patience ..." Mr. Rumsfeld is an experienced politician who can identify any weakness in a question and exploit it to dodge the central issue. In this case, he did just that and started his answer off with "I don't agree with the premise of your question, I didn't make the decision to go to war." That may be technically correct—the fault rests fully with the president, but his answer was designed to lead the audience to believe he was not involved. Everyone knows that the Secretary of Defense would naturally be involved in such decisions—and his opinion would weigh heavily on a president's decision to begin combat operations.

Because of the confrontational nature of my question, the generals who were accompanying Mr. Rumsfeld on his royal progress through Iraq, were upset and glared at me through the rest of the event. But there was nothing they could do about it—he had opened the floor up to questions and I asked one. My only hope is that I soured, however slightly, his final official trip to Iraq.

An interesting aside about that visit is that all of the soldiers who were present at Mr. Rumsfeld's town-hall meeting were *disarmed*. Military Police used hand-held metal detectors to make sure that no one had weapons of any kind. Imagine that, several hundred soldiers, in the middle of a combat zone, disarmed because the Secretary of Defense was there. It just seemed bizarre to me that the civilian leader of the military doesn't trust the soldiers. What would the NRA have said about that? Maybe we could ask Sean Hannity, he would know—and he was there.

After that incident, I became infamous around the FOB. But a few weeks later, in January, I was in the Dining Facility (simply called "D-FAC"), and someone came up to me and asked me if I was "The lieutenant who asked Donald Rumsfeld a question." So, I thought to myself, "This is it—I'm going to get shot right here in the D-FAC", but he wanted to shake my hand. He said that despite how the crowd at the event reacted, I was not the only person who felt that way about Rumsfeld. I don't know the person's name or his rank because it was January and he was wearing his fleece jacket, which does not contain a rank insignia or nametape. While I hadn't anticipated this type of support, it was nice to hear. I think that this shows that there were definitely soldiers in the theater that don't agree with this war and are horribly disappointed in our civilian leadership (or truly the lack thereof).

Another experience a few weeks later brought the absurdity of the war into sharp focus. It was then that my commander, who is a staunch, conservative, evangelical-Christian, GOP, supporter of the war, agreed that Mr. Rumsfeld's answer was pretty "chickenshit" (of course this was *after* Rumsfeld had left office). In my commander's view, Rumsfeld knew the meaning of the question, but just picked out anything he could find to avoid personal responsibility for the disaster he helped to create. As I reflect back on this experience, I think that my commander's response sums up Mr. Rumsfeld's, and this entire Administration's approach, planning, and execution of this war: It's chickenshit—*and you just can't make this shit up.*

I want to make an observation about my commander's view of the war. He *was* a staunch supporter of American involvement in Iraq. But I remember *the day,* when, in my opinion, he lost faith in American leadership. He came into the office—for a normal Groundhog Day of same-old, same-old. After his morning staff meeting with the PRT leaders, he read an article I had forwarded to him about a "trench" the U.S. Army was planning to construct around Baghdad. Everyone who read the article instantly saw the absurdity in that idea, and my commander was no exception. He asked, "What are they thinking?"

I asked sarcastically, "Why don't they try building a moat?" My commander suggested that they use the Army's tradition of making an acronym out of everything and actually call it a MOAT: "Mother Of All Trenches". After that he never regained faith in our efforts in Iraq, because he knew that our leaders had lost touch with reality. He also said, "I'm done. I can be packed in 45 minutes."

*   *   *   *

When our replacements arrived in March, everyone was naturally very excited, even the new guys. We were excited to be going home and they were excited to get their tours started. Our unit went immediately to work training the new arrivals. I thought I would have almost two weeks to train the various people doing different parts of my job (the new unit was desperately understaffed, and the commander did not have an Executive Officer, so he farmed out my duties to several people). After two days, I was told that I needed to pack—the 3rd Infantry Division was arriving for the Surge and they needed some people to set up their Civil Affairs support. My commander was tagged by the Battalion Commander for that duty, and he tagged me. So, two days later, I was fully packed and on a plane to Baghdad for the Surge.

I had been to Baghdad once before, on that mission to learn my way around and to badge the BBA's. This visit to the capital was far from normal, this trip was surreal. The Civil Affairs Brigade was set up on Camp Slayer. I preferred to call it the Slayer Fitness Resort. People would stop their daily work to run in the perfect weather. It was March and the weather was very nice, and everywhere you went there were luxurious palaces (although some had been bombed out) surrounded by lakes and palm trees. It was noticeably quiet because there were very few generators (in Mosul the constant rumbling of the huge generators faded into the background and you didn't even notice them, except by their absence).

We were housed in a bungalow on a man-made lake full of large carp. My commander would fish in the morning from the back ledge—right out the sliding glass door of his room, which overlooked the lake. People would fish in the middle of the day all around these lakes. The place was amazing, but I'm glad that I didn't spend my entire tour there. After seeing how Civil Affairs in Baghdad lives, I'm glad I experienced at least a little bit of comparative hardship by going to Mosul.

When the 3rd Infantry Division finally arrived, we quickly turned things over to their permanent Civil Affairs unit and got the hell out of Dodge. We did not want to stick around for even one extra minute, in case someone got the great idea of extending our tours.

*   *   *   *

At this point, I believe it would be appropriate for me to make an observation about the Surge. Before the war, the Chief of Staff of the Army, General Eric Shinseki, testified before Congress that his professional assessment was such that "I would say that what's been mobilized to this point—something on the order of several hundred thousand soldiers—are probably, you know, a figure that would be required."[4]

The Administration, and the Neoconservatives who developed this intellectually bankrupt policy, didn't like that answer because they calculated that it could harm the public's assent to the war. So they fired him. The most senior officer in the Army spoke his honest professional opinion—he did his *duty* by telling Congress what it needed to hear—and he was fired for his honesty.

With the benefit of hindsight, General Shinseki's correct assessment is obvious for all to see. We have on the order of several hundred thousand people occupying Iraq right now, when you include the profiteering contractors doing the jobs traditionally reserved for soldiers.

In the end, his assessment of the need for more troops was adopted with the advent of the Surge. It was a belated admission that we had too few troops in the beginning. If his advice had been heeded from the beginning, one of two things probably would have been the result: 1) we wouldn't have invaded (because the public wouldn't have supported it), which is probably too far fetched to have any credibility, or 2) the insurgency wouldn't have taken hold to the extent that it did or lasted as long. More soldiers early on would have been available to crush it during its infancy—and to prevent the looting which occurred in the weeks immediately after "Mission Accomplished". Our failure to use a force large enough to occupy the country armed the resistance with weapons that are still haunting us today.

But the fact is we used too few troops in order to test, by gambling the blood of American servicemen and women, the theory of preemptive war. The Administration—and the American people—lost that gamble. Because the good general's assessment of the situation was finally adopted and more troops committed, those that failed to follow the advice of the military experts before the war, *have no right to claim credit if the Surge eventually proves successful.* Their theory is completely discredited and any success can only be attributed to the ultimate realization and acceptance of the facts on the ground. Their ivory-tower theories of the use of force, and implementation by a morally and intellectually challenged president, are forever discredited. And they cannot be allowed to seize any credit for making, four years too late, decisions that should have been made *before* Shock and Awe.

∗   ∗   ∗   ∗

Our small unit finally made it to Kuwait and two days later we were on a plane back to the States. We arrived at Ft. Dix, NJ, on Easter Sunday 2007 and were warmly welcomed home by members of the Veterans of Foreign Wars (VFW). A few hours later, we were on a bus headed to Ft. Bragg.

We knew that we would be housed in Old Division for about a week. After Iraq, Old Division was simply *intolerable*. Some of us rented cars and got rooms by the week off post. Out processing should have taken no more than one week, but it was stretched out because Warrior Brigade (we still called it that despite its name change) would not communicate with other commands on post—commands that had to do paperwork. We finally had to take things into our own hands and go directly to the Civil Affairs Command to get the final release paperwork done. If we hadn't done that, one necessary piece of paper would have made us stay an extra five days (because Warrior Brigade routinely took three day passes—taking off Mondays—and leaving at noon on Fridays, so they only got three full days of work each week). To Warrior Brigade, the influx of over one thousand returning reservists from Iraq and Afghanistan didn't amount to enough work to warrant a full 40 hours a week in the office.

We arrived at Ft. Bragg on a Sunday. By Thursday, we had sat through a few days of out-briefings and we were waiting on one piece of paper to schedule our physicals. But we had no idea when we would get that piece of paper. That same Thursday afternoon, people from Afghanistan deployments began to arrive. They asked us how things were going and how long they should expect to be there. One of our sergeants stated bluntly, "Get comfortable. You're gonna be here awhile. The only advice I can give is to start drinking heavily." *You can't make this shit up.*

On April 25, 2007, I finally arrived back in Salt Lake City. My Mesopotamian misadventure had come to a close at last. On June 13, I sent in, once again, my resignation paperwork. I had submitted my original resignation in August 2001, but the Army never processed it, and that's how I got caught in their net for this deployment. I received my formal—and final—discharge notification on August 25, 2007, stating that my commission and all appointments had been vacated. I am now free to never again fight in illegal wars for the benefit of profiteering cronies.

Before I left Mosul, I wrote a letter home to my friends and family. Here is a part of it:

March 5, 2007: In a few days I will part from friends—family really—that I have made here. And I will most likely never see them again. So there is a feeling of finality to what is happening. This war is a chapter in my life that I had hoped would never be written, and now that the major part of it is over, I can't possibly express the joy of seeing it end, but I can't reconcile that with the feeling of loss. I have lost something indescribable here. If I had to explain it, I would have to think of it as losing a part of my cherished liberalism. I have become colder because of this experience. When you next see me, I will look a little different (believe it or not I have gained weight here), but I think that you will find the change in my personality to be even more striking. I hope I can regain what I have lost, but somehow it feels like a shift in my core from which I will not recover.

I thought that time would fade the images of Mosul from my memory, but if so it is going to take some time. The blazing heat, the bright sun, the dust, the mud, the sweat: Endless Groundhog Days.

GAYS IN THE MILITARY

I take a wide stance on the issue of gays in the military. My position is simple: The Don't Ask Don't Tell policy is unfair, unjust, directly harms our national security, and must be repealed to allow gays to serve openly. I believe I have proven by my example that the job can be done by gay people. But my part in the war was very insignificant; there are much better examples to be found among the countless gay people doing really important jobs for our national security—and in uniform—such as Linguists, Intelligence Analysts, Military Police, doctors, lawyers, the list is endless.

When I first set out to write this book, I made an outline of all the things I thought would need to be included to make my case for gays serving in the military. I was going to include a history of the Don't Ask Don't Tell policy, attempt to refute the rationale for it with evidence from other writers, argue the moral points presented by religious leaders who support it, and even give examples of other developed countries' policies about gays in uniform. However, as I began my research, I realized that so much of that has already been done; there is not much I can add to that substantial body of work. So, I have decided to appeal to my reader's sense of decency, common sense, and fairness—and concern for our national security. In short, I am going to use logic and emotion (and hopefully a little humor) to make my points.

If someone were going to make an argument condemning another policy, such as racial segregation for example, that person would not need to recite a comprehensive history of racism in order to make a forceful case against it. One need only look to the injustice of it. I believe Americans have a good enough grasp of contemporary history to forego a scholarly historical account of Don't Ask Don't Tell, and will appreciate and understand my succinct frontal assault on this unjustifiable and unjust policy.

During my tour in Iraq, I did at times go out of my way to sow seeds of suspicion about my orientation, but that was more to make a point than to try to use it to my advantage. After all, I could have, at virtually any time, said "I am gay", and been on a plane out of Iraq within days. But I didn't. The Don't Ask Don't Tell policy was in place when I first joined the Army and I knew then that being gay is irrelevant to being a soldier. I am not a hypocrite and it would have taken a vast amount of hypocrisy to use being gay to get out of a deployment, when that fact was irrelevant at the time I joined.

Throughout this chapter I will provide examples of how I pushed the envelope, so to speak, with regard to the Don't Ask Don't Tell policy. Some people could (and probably will) come to the conclusion, based upon these examples, that the policy works. Such an argument would probably go something like this: "As long as he wasn't asked, and as long as he didn't tell, he was able to be himself." That is partly true, but you have to consider the fact that I literally *didn't care* if someone found out I'm gay. I lived on the edge of the policy because I had the luxury of doing so. The Army is not my life (remember I was called back from Fort Living-Room because the Army is short on personnel). But many other gay people actually like the military life and are dedicated to their jobs. The policy denies them the comfort of being themselves; they endure years of oppression so that they can do what they love to do: Serve their country—and then retire.

While many of my senior officers didn't care, unlike the Administration and high brass, it isn't because I didn't give many good reasons for them to suspect me of being gay. One colleague called me "reckless" for the way I sometimes acted. I was by no means flamboyant, but I didn't attempt at all to hide who I am. I lived by a personal policy, which was never tested, whereby if I had been directly asked, I would have told. In fact, there are several times I all but did, in rather humorous fashion. The examples that I share with you will illustrate the point that I was able to walk right up to the line—and no one cared.

*   *   *   *

In Iraq, I had an SUV assigned to me. It was an up-armored Toyota Land Cruiser. One day I was driving when my passenger, who was giving me directions, told me to "Go straight at the stop sign". I told him "I will go forward. I don't like to go straight".

*   *   *   *

The arguments against Don't Ask Don't Tell are so obvious and strong that I will not even try to develop new and better ones. I will undoubtedly repeat arguments the reader has seen many times. But I hope that you will develop a new appreciation for the unfairness of the policy as it is demonstrated by my personal experiences and observations—in a combat zone.

There are several concepts that I will lead you through in my discussion of the policy. I will of course speak of the inherent unfairness of it, but I will also address the generational divide making the policy irrelevant, and finally lead you through the unexpected weaknesses this creates in our country's quest for national security.

But before I do that, I want to address one underlying assumption of the policy. That assumption is of "choice" in human sexual preference. The policy is undoubtedly—and admittedly—based upon the assumption that being gay is a choice. In truth, the only choice that a gay person makes is the choice of whether to live his life in happiness as nature made him, or to live in misery by adhering to someone else's definition of morality. The obvious choice for anyone is to follow their heart.

During my tour in Iraq, the serious topic of gays in the military would sometimes come up. We were, after all, in the middle of a war with an Army stretched dangerously thin. So, officers would debate policy (knowing, of course, that we had no power to actually influence anything, but we engaged in the conversations nonetheless). Debates that I participated in on many controversial topics would usually take place in the dining facility with officers and sergeants from many different units.

When the topic of gays in the military would be raised (usually by a joke of some kind—and never by me), everyone implicitly agreed that gays were and are serving and that the Army needed every person we could get. When possible, I would always try to take the more subtle argument on the side of letting gays openly serve, because "they" have served in every campaign fought by every military in history since at least Alexander the Great. The policy doesn't actually stop them from serving, it just makes them second-class citizens while doing so.

Inevitably, when talking about gays in the military, some people will revert to the tired argument that being gay is a choice. To that argument, I would always ask if they felt that they chose to be straight. I would usually get an answer of "Yes", so then I ask if they believe that they could choose to have sex with a guy. The answer was usually "No". But in one surprising instance, an officer who was trying to make a point said, "If I had to, I could probably force myself to have sex with a guy." Keep in mind that that is an argument that was forbidden to me (I was a single guy who didn't have a girlfriend, etc.), so I could never have used it. But that was exactly the opening I needed, because most people have never heard the argument I was about to unleash on this unwitting audience.

That officer, everyone knew, was playing devil's advocate. But he didn't realize that he had given me the perfect opening by stating that he felt he could "force" himself to have sex with a guy. That is, to make the "choice" to be gay. What that statement betrayed is a lack of understanding of how human sexuality works. I can understand the confusion because human sexuality is not very well under-stood even by those who make a career of studying it. However, it is undoubtedly true that anyone could have sex with anyone else, as has been proven in prisons and military barracks for centuries. It is physically possible for two people, regardless of their orientation, to be sexually intimate with each other. But to "force" oneself to the "choice" of having gay sex misses this important point: While it may be possible to force yourself to the *act* of sex, it is impossible for you to force yourself to the *desire* for it. And that is the root of our sexuality—our desire for the touch.

With these observations, it is not hard to conclude that sexual orientation is irrelevant in professional environments. The military prides itself on being one such professional environment. Senior leaders from Generation X and later have mostly worked in the modern professional business world (or the Guard or Reserve) and are used to the idea of gays being a part of society. Younger soldiers don't care: They've served with gays, grew up with gays, have gays in their fami-lies or as close friends—or might even be gay themselves. *Most* people simply don't care, and military professionals in a war zone are smart enough to recognize the importance of keeping a valuable asset that won't be replaced if removed. Proof of the irrelevancy of sexual orientation in hiring is confirmed by the fact that the corporate professional world has become increasingly gay friendly over the past decade.

*   *   *   *

I have included the actual wording of the Don't Ask Don't Tell policy, as set by statute in 10 USC Section 654, in the Appendices[1]. But I begin my assault by stating plainly that the Don't Ask Don't Tell policy is a stain on the credibility of the American Republic. It is most easily assailed from the standpoint of the pride and history that America has as an inclusive nation that values freedom above all else. First off, by virtue of the very way that the policy is worded and applied, not all citizens are equal. From a constitutional perspective, equality is a vital principle so important that it has been enshrined in the 13th and 14th Amendments. Secondly, the historical and traditional evidence of the importance of "Equal Justice Under Law" can be seen written on the stones capping the building of our nation's highest court. And yet with evidence written in stone, and enshrined in our sacred documents, the Don't Ask Don't Tell policy still exists, despite the fact that it fails to reconcile with our nation's proclaimed beliefs.

The policy doesn't just contradict our principles; it proves to be even more insidious. You see, the policy not only allows the government to discriminate, it actually *requires* the government to discriminate. We have many laws in our country that seek to ban discrimination, but Don't Ask Don't Tell specifically requires such discrimination against an identifiable group of citizens: Gays.

If you take the time to read the formal writing of the statute, you will notice that Congress falls back on its constitutional authority to create the rules of discipline for the U.S. Armed Forces. I would like you to pay special attention to these passages:

(a) (4) The primary purpose of the armed forces is to prepare for and to prevail in combat should the need arise.

(a) (5) The conduct of military operations requires members of the armed forces to make extraordinary sacrifices, including the ultimate sacrifice, in order to provide for the common defense.

Notice that the law explicitly recognizes the sacrifice required of individuals serving in uniform. Then notice that the policy, within a few lines, disregards this and falls back on "tradition" by stating:

(a) (13) The prohibition against homosexual conduct is a longstanding element of military law that continues to be necessary in the unique circumstances of military service.

Well, which is it? Does the military exist to be prepared to prevail in war or does it exist to be a social engineering experiment designed around discrimination? Congress can't have it both ways. You can't credibly claim on the one hand that the ultimate sacrifice may be asked for, and then on the other hand state that prejudice based on tradition indicates that an identifiable group isn't worthy of that sacrifice.

Notice that the law couches itself in abstractions such as:

(a) (6) Success in combat requires military units that are characterized by high morale, good order and discipline, and unit cohesion.

Good order and discipline is essential, yes. No one argues about that. But the policy has nothing to do with good order and discipline—it has to do with *fear*. Fear of gays serving openly in the military. I find it interesting how so much of what our government does today revolves around fear: Fear of terrorism is used to drive us to the point of barbarity (torturing people); and fear of each other is used to drive us apart as a country. Despite what the statute says, I find it very hard to believe that those in the highest reaches of our government are doing everything in their power to "prevail" as quickly as possible. The extension of this war into the years, rather than months, gives forceful proof of the fearful machinations of our politicians.

The excerpts I have cited from the law do not address this question: Where did this policy come from? While the official military and legal explanation is unit cohesiveness and morale, my personal observations tell me otherwise. You see our "brave" senior leaders (senior military officers and civilian officials) who argue in favor of the policy are afraid of gays. Pure and simple, it is fear that drives them. At this point you're probably saying "Gee, Gary, thanks for the news flash." And you would be right to do so. I'm not telling you anything that you haven't heard before.

Fear is a natural human emotion, but military training is supposed to teach you how to swallow your fear and face enemy machine guns. That's the whole purpose of Basic Training: To teach you to follow orders and do what needs to be done regardless of the cost to yourself because others are counting on you. Yet we have military leaders whose personal surrender to fear leads them to support the retention of Don't Ask Don't Tell.

Let me highlight this: Senior officers should feel emotion, but allowing fear to dictate policy is most unbecoming of a leader—especially a military one. These are men and women (mostly men) who are specifically charged with facing down fear and yet they hide behind this policy—a policy which allows them the cover to cower from that which is not a real threat.

The cowardice and hypocrisy of our "leaders" is apparent on its face. These people ask Americans to be patient to see if their failed policies will somehow miraculously turn around, while at the same time advancing other policies which directly hinder our national security efforts. Our government under Bush/ Cheney is obsessed with fear. They use fear to sustain every failed policy. And the basis for the unjust homophobic Don't Ask Don't Tell policy is fear founded on outdated moral outrage that gays should be here at all. They know that, in time, they are going to lose on the greater issues of gay rights and they want to forestall that for as long as they can.

George W. Bush was afraid to go to Vietnam. When his country needed him, and he was a fully trained Air Force fighter pilot, he chose instead to look after his own interests by getting out of the National Guard—and going to work for a political campaign. Dick Cheney had "other priorities" (FIVE times) than fighting for his country in a time of national emergency. That doesn't sound too patriotic to me. Nor does it sound like they should be given any deference on the issues of national security and military policy. They both could have faced America's enemies where and when it counted—on the ground in Vietnam. Yet these two cowards make and enforce the war decisions that weaken us all.

*   *   *   *

In January, a member of my Battalion's Headquarters Company sent an e-mail to all members, inviting everyone available to a Super Bowl party. Being a smartass, and playing on the stereotype that gays don't like sports, I hit the reply-to-all and sent the following message: "Is this some sort of sporting event?" A colonel wrote back (also, by reply-to-all), that if I continue in my lack of sports enthusiasm, he was "Going to order me to wear a pink tutu and dance during the half-time show". I replied to the colonel (and ONLY to the colonel), "Sir, you have no idea how much I would enjoy that."

*   *   *   *

Some officers agree with former General Peter Pace in calling homosexuality "immoral" and believe that is a good enough reason to keep the policy. Yet, even with this claim, the military grants thousands of "moral waivers" each year in order fill the ranks. These moral waivers aren't allowed for gay soldiers, they are designed to allow people with criminal records (sometimes felonies) to fill the ranks. So much for the morality argument. I am in no way arguing against allowing people with criminal records to serve; once a person has paid his/her debt to society, full rights of citizenship should be restored, but that argument will have to wait for another day.

Not all officers fall into the Peter Pace mold, however. General officers such as former Army Chiefs of Staff General Peter Schoomaker and General Erik Shinseki both have argued for at least a re-evaluation of the policy. They rightly recognize that we need to fight this war smartly. In order to that we need to be careful not to base our national security on the simple-minded prejudice of fundamentalist zealots.

I know you must be asking yourself, "Where is he getting all of this from?" As remarkable as it sounds, all of these arguments were made for me by former Wyoming Senator Alan K. Simpson in an editorial he wrote for the Washington Post in March of 2007[2]. An important point the senator makes in his piece is that he voted *for* the policy in 1993, but now he wants to see it abolished, because he recognizes the threat it creates. Like I stated from the beginning, I'm not offering any new arguments against this policy, I am simply pointing out what others have said before. I can put it no better than the senator himself when he concluded his article:

> *"This policy has become a serious detriment to the readiness of America's forces as they attempt to accomplish what is arguably the most challenging mission in our long and cherished history."*

But this doesn't conclude *my* chapter on the topic. I must make the reader understand *why* this policy is a detriment to the United States. Just quoting a former senator (even one from as conservative a state as Wyoming) isn't enough to accomplish the task. To understand military life, and those who make it up, is to understand that soldiers talk about sex *all the time*. Fear enters the equation for our senior military leaders because of their culturally instilled discomfort from an earlier age pertaining to gay relationships. Essentially, the matter comes down to senior leaders who are accustomed to overhearing a young man say to his friends, "I'd like to fuck that chick", fear hearing a young man say, "I'd like to fuck that guy". These older officials fear that openly gay soldiers will be, well, *openly gay*. Apparently they feel that preventing openly gay soldiers from serving is less detrimental to a unit's readiness than the loss of, oh, let's say an Arabic translator.

The Don't Ask part is nice for these senior leaders, but it's the Don't Tell part that matters to them most. While everyone else is talking openly about their lives and who they are—sharing of themselves as a means to create community or *cohesiveness* within the unit—the U.S. Military explicitly forces gays to disengage from this fundamental unit cohesion process.

I don't want anyone to read this and think that our soldiers are just a bunch of sex-maniacs roaming the streets of foreign countries. What I'm illustrating here is a response to the awful oppression that *is* war. Talking, including talking about loved ones and relationships, is an essential part of relieving the stress that comes from living in a war zone. Such expressions also bring members of a unit closer together, by allowing them to share in the details of each other's lives.

Imagine for a moment that you made a phone call home from a combat zone and had a fight with your significant other (yes, spats happen even when you're half a world away) and you hang up the phone upset from the conversation. Your buddy just did the same thing and he's spouting off about how his girlfriend said this and did that. But you can't vent like he can because you can't say, "My boyfriend …", you would have to hide it by maybe saying "My girlfriend …" What's the significance of that you might ask? What happens when your buddy asks you your "girlfriend's" name?

You see, by forcing gays to remain "in the closet" regarding an important part of their lives (talking about their personal relationships), the policy actually *prevents* unit cohesion, by preventing everyone from having an equal part in the community that is the unit. This keeps them as second-class citizens, with a secret that they have to keep from everyone out of fear of losing their job, or more distressingly, their honor.

Well, just in case our military leaders haven't noticed, gays *are* serving. That is why the concept of the policy itself is openly ridiculed in the military in a variety of ways. An example of this can be heard at least once a day on an active duty Army post. Soldiers often say the words, "Don't Ask Don't Tell" after someone says or does something that a stereotypical gay person would say or do. And soldiers have a playful disdain for the policy as well. So much so, that they will toy with it, openly. Here's an example: Every member of my unit in Iraq had to choose a personal handle for radio communications. One young soldier (who is straight, by the way) chose as his handle "Brokeback". He was able to keep it for only a few days before those in command figured out what it meant and made him change it.

The policy has been in place for so long that most mid-level officers and sergeants have no actual military experience without it (I fall into this category). But even those among the older generations of soldiers and officers, many of which were called back from the Inactive Reserve, are not immune to being taken in by using the nature of the policy playfully.

Once again, I rely on my personal experiences where the policy manifested in everyday social interaction. If you'll recall from my earlier Deployment chapter, I was housed for training in the condemned good ol' Building 5058 on Ft. Bragg's Old Division. During this period of so-called "training", one of the officers bought a huge hard rubber dildo. This wasn't your average sized rubber phallus, it was obscenely large. I dare say it was gargantuan. Think Godzilla on Viagra and you've got the image. I'm graphic to drive home the point here. This was every-day life in the military.

Back to the story. During the idle time while waiting for deployment, the officers in my barracks made good use of this dildo. It would come out when someone would fall asleep and would be placed in compromising positions with the sleeping victim, in order for pictures to be taken. It even accompanied some-one on deployment, with the intent that it be handed off to former residents of Building 5058 as we met each other in Iraq. It never made it to me, but I under-stand that several people did find it in their possession at one point or another during their tours. I even heard a rumor that it made its way from Iraq to Afghanistan somehow, but I could never confirm that.

I don't think it was the intent of those who wielded the dildo, but their actions illustrate the absurdity of the policy. Any policy mocked so openly, such as this one, is doomed to fail. That is the real point here: The generalized careless attitude people have toward homosexuality in the military today proves that it has failed. It is, or at least should be, only a matter of time before the brass recog-nizes it. It is far past time for them to wake up to this realization; inertia is the only real reason that the policy is still in force.

*   *   *   *

During my deployment I drove my Toyota Land Cruiser everywhere around the FOB. One day, while driving to lunch, a friend asked me what kind of car I drive at home. I told him I drive a Saturn. He then asked if it was a manual or automatic. I told him I drive a stick, "Because there's nothing like having a shaft in your hand."

*   *   *   *

Open criticism of leaders is not allowed in the military. Therefore, since the policy is officially supported by the leadership, the only safe way for the soldiers to criticize it—consciously or otherwise—is through the use of irony and humor. This use of humor shields the soldiers in their attack of the policy, just as a Court Jester was shielded not only by his role, but by the use of humor to illustrate the Court's flaws. The playful mocking of the policy blunts the criticism of leader-ship as it is directed toward other soldiers of the same rank. At the same time it demonstrates that the enforcement of the policy is inherently flawed. Just as a leader cannot long survive the undermining of his authority by ridicule from subordinates, neither can a policy long survive the ridicule of those it is supposed to govern. At least that is what we would like to think. However, even with the moral authority of the policy eroded as it is, it is not within the power of the military hierarchy to repeal it. That responsibility rests solely with Congress.

There are a number of reasons why the policy has met such subversive resistance. The first among these in my view is the generational divide between the old guard leaders who had no experience with openness about sexuality in general (not just the gay sex), and the new generation who have grown up in a world much more evolved in its attitudes and understanding of sexuality. The following example illustrates this generational divide quite well.

I had been laying on my bunk for almost six weeks with no training, when I was finally assigned to the 403rd Civil Affairs Battalion for final train-up for deployment. One day, my company was resting while awaiting another training event when several of the soldiers started talking about porn. They were comparing the artistic nature of 70's & 80's porn to that of more recent productions. The young specialists and privates believed that the newer films were superior, while the senior sergeant engaged in the conversation believed that the prowess of the male actors in the 70's & 80's outshined anything from today. To make his point, the sergeant noted that most guys in new porn shave their chests, balls and asses. The generational divide became apparent when one younger soldier piped in that he shaved *his* chest and balls and others noted that they also shaved theirs'. The sergeant, being older, looked at them with some suspicion and began to speak of it not being manly, etc. when one of the soldiers said, "Sergeant, our generation just considers it to be cleaner." The sergeant's response was, "What am I, a caveman?"

For me this exchange, and the differing opinions of manliness held by the sergeant and the younger enlisted soldiers, exposes the generational divide within military culture (and arguably American culture at large). First, the soldiers were still talking about sex, as they always do, but the criteria by which masculinity was evaluated had shifted. The shift moved literally from the caveman physicality most associated with masculinity—hairiness—to a clean shaven modern view. No man wants his woman to be hairy, so in the caveman's view, smoothness was associated with the female. Therefore, when the younger generation specifically embraces this key quality of what is traditionally feminine (the aspect of smooth, hairless skin), it illustrates a clear shift in thinking.

The younger generation, by asserting cleanliness as a motive for shaving, has decoupled hairiness as an aspect of male sexuality from that which was previously viewed as distinctly male. This is only one illustration of a continuously evolving thought on manliness. However, the evolution does demonstrate the potential for continued mindset shifts regarding male sexuality as more and more people from younger generations join the military's ranks. Were one to follow this line of reasoning, it would be obvious that over time the policy would be repealed de facto by the ever decreasingly subtle defiance of the policy by younger and younger military generations. But more directly on point, we do not have the luxury of waiting that long. History is full of examples of bad ideas that stayed around well past their time, to the detriment of those forced to live under them. If the reader will remember, we are at war and still desperately need soldiers now—even gay ones!

I am not making the assertion that simply because younger soldiers shave their privates (wow, no pun intended there) they are more openly accepting of homosexuals. I relate this experience because it demonstrates the fact that societal views on sexuality are continuously evolving. As the military is part of society—though separated in significant ways—it should therefore come as no surprise that the sexual attitudes of military personnel would evolve. However, this evolution has expanded to include acceptance of homosexuals. Polling shows that the vast majority of younger soldiers are tolerant of serving side-by-side with gays[3]. This means they don't mind sharing a foxhole or barracks with gay people. What about the showers, you ask? Showers are mostly private in the military now. The younger generation's acceptance most likely stems from their social experiences, where they have interacted with gay people at school and parties. Furthermore, in the crucible of junior high and high school gym class, nascent soldiers would have had to take showers with other students, knowing (or at least suspecting) someone was gay. And yet they suffered no ill effects.

The Don't Ask Don't Tell policy allegedly maintains good order and discipline and/or unit cohesion. But, even if this were true, it is not the gay person that would create any disturbance, it is the reaction to his presence of those around him. Therefore, the policy imposes a penalty upon gay service members for being who they are, while protecting bald-faced prejudice. Justice in our society is based upon what a person actually does, not what he *may* do, nor does our concept of justice hold someone accountable for the reactions others *might* have towards him. This policy is thus conceptually no different than the shameful racial segregation of our past. Fortunately, as noted above, a generational shift on these attitudes is occurring *now*.

It employs essentially the same logic that makes fundamentalist Muslim governments require women to wear burkas—that logic being that men cannot control themselves with regard to women, so it is a woman's responsibility to negate a man's reaction to her. In other words, *the woman is ultimately responsible for how a man may react to her presence.* Thus she must cover herself. The Don't Ask Don't Tell policy, far from being a policy that maintains order and a strong military, is nothing more than a shameful burka shrouding our proud gay troops.

Let me appropriately end the discussion of the evolution of soldiers' attitudes towards sexuality with a reference to a locker room. That is where most of the emotion behind this policy comes from: Some deep-seeded male heterosexual fear that another man might look at him in the shower and find him attractive. That's mostly where the "tradition" of the policy comes from—locker room speculation about gay sex by insecure high school jocks, some of whom are now in uniform. To conclude my refutation of your locker room fears guys, let me just say this: Get over yourself, Bubba! Stop flattering yourself. You really aren't all that good looking.

The open ridicule of the policy by soldiers is not the only evidence of the policy's failures. I come back again to the inescapable reality that there are homosexuals everywhere in the military. Commanders can make life for any soldier bearable or miserable—it all depends on style. One of my commanders had real style. He led through respect—up and down the chain. He was the perfect example of a leader, as far as I am concerned. The way he acted in command is how I had always pictured myself acting, if I found myself in command. I respect him deeply to this day. Though we disagreed on almost everything, I consider him a close friend.

He is married, with children and active in his Southern Baptist church. I know many of the lefties reading this book will jump to certain conclusions based on his religious affiliation, owing to the fact that Pat Robertson is the poster-boy for it. I caution you against this. He proved one thing to me that I would never have believed before meeting him: Some Southern Baptists are actually Christians, living by the teachings of Christ, not the rhetoric from the vitriolic pulpits.

He is a stoic in the classical sense. So much so, that he has distilled and adopted a stoic personal motto: "It is what it is." He repeated that statement whenever circumstances were less than optimal for our missions. This motto certainly describes stoicism in its most basic form. Now, I know that some people might try to use such an argument to reinforce Don't Ask Don't Tell: "It is what is, so why not accept it?" Like with almost everything else, there are two sides to that line of stoic reasoning. Gay people exist and live their lives like everyone else.

We should be—and increasingly are—accepted. It is what it is, so why should the policy be in place?

✳   ✳   ✳   ✳

In November, we had a journalist come to stay with us for a few weeks. He was doing a piece on the Field Artillery unit that was supporting the PRT. He was in his early 20's (at least he looked that way) and very good looking, and kept his long hair meticulously in a distressed metrosexual fashion. He came into the Operations office a few days after I got back from my Italian leave. While he was standing in the door talking to another officer, I caught myself gazing longingly at him. I know the officer saw me doing it, because when the journalist left, I turned to look at him and he pointed at me accusingly and said, "No!" I couldn't leave it at that and said, "He's going to need a place to stay. He can bunk with me!"

✳   ✳   ✳   ✳

I was fortunate to be surrounded by officers who understood the policy and followed it to the letter. I did walk right up to the line, but no one asked and I didn't tell, though I wanted to, if just to prove the point that gays can do the job. In fact, throughout my tour in Iraq, a fellow officer proclaimed several times, "When we get back to Bragg, I'm going to buy you dinner and ask you some questions." I was open to that suggestion, and after we got back to Ft. Bragg, we went out to a restaurant and over wine I cut him off at the pass—outing myself. He said he suspected all along, and of course I knew that. And he knew that I knew that he knew.

This is what I was talking about earlier, about the community—or unit cohesion—that the policy prevents. Here was an officer with whom I had spent a whole year and forged a friendship in fire, yet I could not be open with him during the tour—I had to wait until a few days before we were to return to our normal lives to be honest with him. It is irrelevant that he suspected I might be gay during the tour. What is relevant is that I couldn't fully participate in unit cohesive activity because of a policy that would prefer I not exist.

I have no military career goals. I have successfully resigned my commission. In fact, I believed I had done so years before being called back. So, the Don't Ask Don't Tell policy was quite immaterial to me. I followed it, of course, but I had some freedom that other gay soldiers don't have: I could push the envelope. It didn't really matter to me if someone found out that I'm gay—it would probably mean going home early, and I was not opposed to that idea at all. But that is beside the point. The point is that I knew many people suspected me of being gay (and I did sometimes go out of my way to help them think that), but it made no difference to them. The job got done, and that's the real measure of a soldier. Just look at how much energy is consumed with such an irrelevant trifle. We're not idly ignoring an 800-pound gorilla in the room; we're actually expending effort to ignore an 800-pound drag queen in the foxhole!

There is a way to measure this energy: Money. Money is an alternative from of energy, it represents the effort required to create goods and services and is the accepted means of their transfer within the economy. Our government spends a quantifiable—and large—amount of energy in the enforcement of Don't Ask Don't Tell. The Government Accountability Office in 2005 attempted to specifically quantify the cost of the policy. The report estimated that between 1994 and 2003, the government spent $95 million to recruit enlisted personnel to replace those who were discharged for being gay[4].

✳   ✳   ✳   ✳

One time I was frustrated at some meddling by a marplot in our unit, who was creating complications, preventing me from completing a necessary task in a timely manner. I stormed into a senior officer's office, looked at him, held my thumb and index finger a millimeter from each other and said, "I am this close to telling you something that's going to *make* you send me home." He knew what I was getting at and responded, "Whoa! Let's not go overboard. What's wrong? What did *Racer-X* do this time?"

✳   ✳   ✳   ✳

I knew that talking about my experiences in Iraq publicly could be problematic for others. As I began the process of writing this book, it occurred to me that there are various people in my former chain of command whose careers could be harmed by my authorship of a Don't Ask Don't Tell-themed book. It would not be impossible (or even very difficult) for someone to look at the personnel roster of our unit and figure out who was who. My name is on the cover of this book and the names of all of those with whom I served in Iraq are in the Army records. I don't want to harm, in any way, the career goals of these people who became as close as family to me. So, I wrote to some people telling them of my intent to write this book and I explained my concerns. I asked for suggestions on how I might prevent any potential damage to their careers for having been senior in rank to me and not pursuing possible suspicions of my sexual orientation. This is part of one letter I received in response (I had to redact some areas to protect the identity of the author):

> *"Here's my recollection—I suspected you may be gay, but I also knew that I could not ask you if you were. Quite frankly, I really did not care and my understanding of the rules was that I can't ask and you can't tell. Write the book—I think I will be covered and will fall on the legal sword if anything comes up. You never came out and I knew not to ask. Sounds pretty straightforward to me ... Thanks for the concern, but I will have plausible deniability due to Don't Ask Don't Tell.*
>
> *The Army is a cross-section of society and all demographics are represented. Here's another effect ... If you were pulled from the position, then you would not have been replaced and [the unit] needed you ... The personnel situation there was akin to stud, not draw, poker. You played the hand you were dealt. You had the respect of the enlisted personnel and that was enough ... They appreciated your candor in always dealing with them honestly and never bullshitting them. They did what you asked because of who you were, not because they were legally bound to do so. You provided positive leadership. Glad you were there."*

You see, corporate America is actually right this time. By rescinding the policy, we will generate a richer and more talented pool of recruits. Fortune 500 companies have accepted that gays are talented and actively recruit them by offering the same benefits they offer their straight employees. These companies understand that to do otherwise will put them at a disadvantage as they pass up talented candidates solely on the basis of sexual orientation—and this allows their competitors to reap the benefits by hiring talented gay employees.

Our military is stretched, by many experts' assessments, to its very breaking point. Yet we have this policy which prevents proud, willing and able gay Americans from openly and courageously sharing in the sacrifice of our national defense. For some people, there is no substitute for military service. Some proponents of the policy point out—correctly—that a gay person can serve openly elsewhere in the U.S. government. That argument misses the point: The traditions and honor that flow from military service cannot be substituted by non-military government service. That's like saying that a postman's uniform is equivalent to a soldier's—and it is not.

Given the shortage of recruits, the military has to expend enormous efforts to find people to enlist. But the Don't Ask Don't Tell policy presents gay people who are out no real motivation to go back into the closet. Some might counter this with something like, "You do what you have to if it's important enough." I would agree with that, and point out that defending the homeland is important enough for the people of the United States to make these collective decisions as well. So, if national defense is important enough, the United States should allow gays to serve.

In times past, gay people may have been willing to make the trade-off between the military and staying in the closet. But that no longer applies to today's individual recruits. As generational attitudes change and gay people come out of the closet younger and younger, it is increasingly unfair and unrealistic to expect them to go back into the closet for a job—even one as important as defending our country.

Contrast my friend's eloquent understanding and recognition of the need for able-bodied soldiers with that of the civilian leadership. We have so many chicken-hawks in this country that love and support war but are too afraid to actually suit up and go fight it themselves. Many of these are the very same people, who, without any military experience, forcefully fall back on the claim that the Don't Ask Don't Tell policy preserves unit discipline; how would they know? They've never been in a unit!

*   *   *   *

One day I was reading my personal e-mail in the PRT Ops office and I remarked that I had received a certificate for $50 off my next purchase at American Eagle Outfitters. An officer in the room asked, "Do you shop there a lot?" I told him, "They have nice jeans for young men. I'm no longer a young man, but that doesn't stop me from going into their stores."

*   *   *   *

Some proponents of the policy say that the military should not be used for social experimentation or engineering. The fact is the jury is already in: Americans at large accept gays living and working along side them. Therefore, the dreaded social engineering cited by these people is actually being foisted upon us by this policy. By refusing to acknowledge what the rest of America already knows to be true, the military is creating a false self-image and harming its effectiveness.

The policy is logically inconsistent with the stated rationale for its existence. Proponents readily admit that gays *are* serving (and always have served) in the military. The policy only prevents the hierarchy of knowing which soldiers are gay, not whether or not gay soldiers are serving. Therefore, the policy explicitly accepts that gays serve. Further, the policy implicitly *allows* gays to serve, although closeted. It logically follows, then, that the policy itself acknowledges that the stated conditions for which it exists ("to maintain good order and discipline and unit cohesion") are deceptive—in that these conditions are presently maintained even with gay people serving. If it were true that gays serving in the military create an actual, verifiable problem relating to good order and discipline or unit cohesion, as argued by the policy, why would *any* policy to allow gays to serve *at all* be tolerable? This inconsistency itself is intolerable in that it creates a second-class citizen soldier. One who must hide an integral part of what makes him who he is in order to proudly fight and protect his family and homeland.

I personally believe that the Don't Ask Don't Tell policy was created as a stepping-stone measure with the unstated goal of integrating openly gay service members into the military. The history of the policy indicates that it was a political compromise, but in the end the ultimate outcome was to create an environment conducive to such integration. The environment is now ripe for the abolishment of this policy. Proof of this can be found in a letter written in November 2007 in which more than two dozen retired generals and admirals "respectfully urge Congress to repeal the Don't Ask, Don't Tell policy"[5].

*   *   *   *

In military writing, most official work is done in a memo format. A well-trained writer who writes for military consumption always remembers the "BLUF principle": Bottom Line Up Front. Therefore I reprise the BLUF statement that I used at the beginning of this chapter: Don't Ask Don't Tell must be repealed.

If, at the end of all the accounts of the policy's injustice, outright ineffectiveness, and failure you still aren't convinced, allow me to put to you another way: The Don't Ask Don't Tell policy harms national security.

There are many actual threats to our national security, and our government should not create more of them in their panic—or perpetuate artificial threats already in existence. The Don't Ask Don't Tell policy puts us in peril in two ways: Directly and indirectly. Since we are, arguably, engaged in a conflict that will last at least one full generation, we need to constantly reevaluate every tactic we employ to ensure that it is effective in the effort to defeat our enemies. Thus, we must ask the following questions concerning every policy decision made: 1) Does this policy strengthen our national security? and 2) Does this policy in any way weaken our enemies? An affirmative response to either question would require that the policy be seriously considered or adopted. But a negative answer to both requires the policy be abandoned. One could only answer "No" to both of those questions regarding Don't Ask Don't Tell.

The policy directly harms our national security by artificially preventing capable and dedicated people from serving in a meaningful and substantive manner. There are many examples of professional men and women being removed from service for no other reason than being gay. But I believe the strongest argument against the policy is confirmed by the dismissal of almost five dozen, 58 to be exact[6], Intelligence Analysts specializing in Arabic translations. These are people who were trained—at great expense—to speak, read, and translate the language of our enemies. They are no longer allowed to do this work because our government believes that adherence to a perverted Right Wing ideology is more important than actually living up to their oaths and using every resource available to defend our homeland.

The policy has an indirect consequence as well: It creates an environment in which someone can be extorted. If the policy did not exist, extortion based upon the fear of losing one's job or honor would not exist. I mentioned honor because being kicked out of the military—for whatever reason—can be viewed by some as a form of personal dishonor. People may react differently to blackmail—and we hope that anyone faced with such a situation would do the right thing, but the right thing is not always apparent to someone being coerced.

The military has a policy which considers an officer with bad credit and/or extensive debt to be a security risk, most likely because money—or lack of it—has the potential to cause lapses in judgment. This policy may make sense, but it is based upon someone's choices and the financial difficulty those choices created for them. The Don't Ask Don't Tell policy is not based upon a choice that someone makes, but instead it is based upon who they are. In the case of poor credit or extensive debt the lure of money can—and has—caused people to act in a manner inconsistent with their duties. In the case of Don't Ask Don't Tell, the policy itself creates such an environment: It has nothing to do with someone's actions or the consequences thereof; the policy itself causes the danger of blackmail.

*   *   *   *

When I took my mid-tour leave in Italy, one of my friends wanted to make sure that I got there safely, so I promised to write to him as soon as I could find a computer. The hostel I stayed at in Rome had one, so I wrote to him the day after I arrived. A few days later, just before I left for Florence, I wrote to him again to let him know how my trip was progressing. I told him of all the pictures I had taken so far and of my visit to the Vatican. When I mentioned the Vatican, I also stated: "As for the Swiss Guards … mmmm their uniforms are very nice."

Another member of my unit who was going to take leave in Italy as well, asked him if he had heard from me. My friend relayed that I was in Rome and enjoying myself, and that I "had a lot of nice things to say about the Swiss Guards." The person asked, "There aren't any women Swiss Guards are there?" to which he had to truthfully answer, "No". The person walked away shaking his head.

*   *   *   *

I have written about the obvious lack of fairness contained within the Don't Ask Don't Tell policy, but that concept of fairness doesn't stop at discrimination against gay soldiers. Let's assume for the moment that the United States were in imminent peril and we, through our elected representatives, decide that we need to begin a military draft (for this, you will obviously need to set aside your knowledge that no one currently in Congress would actually have the spine to do such a thing, regardless of the clear need for it in the face of some serious present threat to our national survival). The Don't Ask Don't Tell policy could potentially give thousands of people an easy way to prevent induction. Thus, only straight people (and gay people who don't tell) would be forced into uniform. Does that sound like sharing the sacrifice when it is most pressing that we do so?

Some may argue that we would simply not allow anyone to get out of service for claiming to be gay. The answer to this argument is apparent: If those claiming to be gay can be forced into service when times are dire, they should be allowed to serve anytime.

Others may argue that we would investigate every claim made of this nature to confirm it. But wouldn't that defeat the whole purpose of a draft? The adoption of a draft, in itself, would indicate that the danger is so imminent that we need to end unnecessary policies and get to the business of training soldiers immediately. That would require the abolition of the discrimination against gays in the military. Why wait for some looming threat to create such a danger when allowing every able-bodied American citizen who wants to serve keep us safer now? Let's not forget those nearly five dozen translators of Arabic who are no longer doing the job.

This is not an academic abstraction. This kind of decision is already being made for us. I was called up, along with thousands of others, for a backdoor draft. One of the units, of which one of my buddies was the Executive Officer, had to kick out a gay soldier just weeks before deploying to Iraq due to the Don't Ask Don't Tell policy. They were already sorely undermanned—like every other deploying unit—and they were forced to deploy with one less desperately needed soldier.

It has been proven that ideology trumps mission accomplishment in the Global War on Terror. Political commissars are prevalent today throughout the federal government. They judge every policy through the spectrum of partisan ideological purity, just like the political officers of the former Soviet Union.

Such commitment and adherence to a strict dogma forces one to wonder if those running our government are truly committed to the cause of national security. I don't believe the American people are committed to war in Iraq any longer (if they ever really were), but we have to ask ourselves, "Now that we're there, shouldn't we be using every last resource to end it quickly?" The only way to do that is to use the best and brightest. That means using everyone willing and able—including gays—in the cause of our defense.

The military does not just need the best and brightest, but also physically fit personnel. Think back to my earlier story of the obese captain recalled to duty from the Inactive Reserve. The U.S. military today is forced to choose between someone whose presence places him and those around him in imminent danger (due to his obesity) and someone who is gay but otherwise physically fit and willing. A person too unfit physically may be unable to perform the rigorous physical duties needed in combat, thus he puts himself and those relying on him in jeopardy. We know how the Army decides this question: The policy forces them to choose the physically unfit person over the gay person solely because of the perverted Right Wing ideology of the civilian authorities.

I believe that we must look deep within ourselves and ask: Is America worth fighting for? I answer "Yes", as I believe every reader of this book would answer. Then of what worth is it to restrict who can fight? Americans all have the same things to defend: Family, friends, and homeland. Do gay Americans, then, have any less to fight for?

If we are to believe our "leaders", the Global War on Terror will have to be fought for a full generation or more before we can defeat our enemies. If that is true, we are obliged to use every resource we have to bring the war to the quickest end. There will be less suffering on all sides if the war ends quickly. Therefore, every American should do what he or she can do in order to achieve our goal: Peace. In order for this to happen, gays must be allowed to serve openly in our military.

*   *   *   *

I think we need to revisit morality for a moment. Many people that support the Don't Ask Don't Tell policy often fall into the "morality" argument, stating that homosexual behavior is an "immoral" choice. As I pointed out at the beginning of this chapter, being gay is not a choice, but having sex is—a choice made by straight people as well as gay people. Regardless of an individual's orientation, having sex is a natural choice that springs from being alive.

Some people actually believe that being gay can be "cured". The flip side of that argument would be to ask, "Can being straight be cured?" To believe that a person can live a lie and be happy is to disregard human nature. And who we love is exclusively determined by the nature of how we love.

Here's the meat and potatoes of it: To the argument that gays shouldn't be in the military because of the morality of their "choice" of orientation, I pose the answer that the decision to go to war itself is a moral choice—and if taken incorrectly and unjustly, it is an immoral one. The point here is, when you have to make a moral choice which results—rightly or wrongly—in a war, you can have no higher moral concern than winning that war. There can be no other priorities. Adhering to the religious fundamentalism of a small minority is not a valid concern and will only hinder our progress toward winning the conflict—and protecting our national interests.

It is American tradition to not only defend the physical hearth and home, but also to defend one's own sense of self—one's personal identity. How can a person be true to his homeland if he is forced to be untrue to himself? This brings me to an important question: Do Americans enjoy liberty because we are a diverse people or are we a diverse people because we enjoy liberty? While I believe these two concepts coexist, the question is nonetheless an important one because it forces us to think about why we defend our country.

Ultimately, disagreement with how gays live their lives is what drives the anti-gay movement. Anyone who does not see the world as these people prescribe or live their lives in the fundamentalist fashion that they dictate, must be scorned and denied respect or status. But in a time of national emergency, when our country is beset not just from foreign menace, but also from domestic threats in the form of our own government, we have to put our individual differences aside and think of America first.

We have been told that the Global War on Terror is paramount to our nation's survival against radical Islamic fundamentalism. But at the same time our government is enforcing a perverted fundamentalist policy against gay Americans. The Don't Ask Don't Tell policy was an ideological curtsey meant to give comfort to the Religious Right in our country: A policy indulgence. It serves no other purpose. It certainly has no national security value, as it actually does us harm and weakens us from within.

This policy of discrimination must be abolished. But the military has no authority or inclination to change it. That authority, both moral and legal, rests with Congress—and with us. It is up to the American people to force our government to do its duty: Protect our homeland with every resource available—including gay Americans.

Farmer's Market

A Farmer's Market is the ultimate ideal of American commerce. It is not high finance in some far-off commercial capital, using sophisticated mathematical models designed around economic efficiency, solely to maximize profit. The Farmer's Market is Americans doing what they have done since before the founding—trading in cottage-industry goods, such as hand-made pottery, tie-dyed hemp T-shirts, corn from their small farms, and even honey from tended hives. Simply put, A Farmer's Market is Americans partaking in the bounty of America.

One such Farmer's Market takes place every Friday during the summer in Laramie, Wyoming. To accommodate this expression of fundamental American commerce, the city closes off some of the main streets for a few hours. During the first summer after my return from Iraq, I received an invitation to speak at the University of Wyoming about my experiences. My sponsor for the event and I went to that weekly Farmer's Market to hand out fliers to encourage the general public to come and hear my speech, and to get involved.

We handed a flier to a lady tending her concession stand and she instantly handed it back stating that she supported the war because one of her sons was on his *third* tour in Iraq. In addition to her son, she had other family members currently serving in the Iraq and Afghanistan theaters of operations. I was surprised, not by her support of the war, but by the extent to which her family was bearing the burden. We chatted politely for a moment, and, in keeping with the overall theme of my speech, we ended our conversation with her by noting that while she and her family were making great sacrifices for our country, we could only wish that the sacrifice was shared by more of the American people.

In the weeks leading up to that speech, I worked through many drafts and spent a great deal of time writing and rewriting it. In those preparations, I drew upon the fact that the year I had spent in Iraq gave me a little credibility to speak about shared sacrifice. My goal for that speech was to outline for my audience (as abstractly as I could) how the American people are not sacrificing for the Global War on Terror. In speaking with that lady at the Farmer's Market, though, I had to acknowledge to myself that the "sacrifice" I had made by spending a year in Northern Iraq was very little compared to what others were sacrificing. Nevertheless, it was a great deal more than the majority of Americans are sacrificing.

To date, the sacrifice most of us have made for the war has been a generalized concern and unease about it. Believe me, I know that Americans are concerned, but that concern, thus far, hasn't translated into much action. For the most part, we sit in our homes and watch the war on the news or read about it online, but it doesn't really touch us in any way that we can actively perceive. However, the war *does* touch us. It lurks in the fear that many of us have of another terrorist attack. We see images of violence across the globe in Baghdad or Mosul, and somewhere in the darkest recesses of our mind, we are grateful that the violence isn't here, but in some abstract "there", far removed from us.

It is that fear seeping from the dark recesses of our American collective sub-conscious that forces us to ask such disturbing, but vital questions as: Would I want the government to abide by the individual protections found in the Constitution if I knew that, by so doing, a terrorist bomb would go off and kill my mom? I can answer for myself the only way I know how: Simply that my mother raised me to fight for my rights. She also taught me that the greater good is always worth the life of one person. So, while I would fight to save her life—or the life of any American from the harm a terrorist would seek to do—I would fight equally hard to save her *liberty*. I derived from my mother's example that her life, my life—and arguably anybody's life—only has meaning as expressed through the exercise of liberty.

Furthermore, I believe that the choice of preserving our constitutional free-doms or protecting ourselves from terrorist attack is a *false* choice. The freedoms found in the Constitution are the greatest security we possess. There can be no choice between liberty and security because they cannot be separated—they are the same thing!

Since my return to "the real world", I have found that life here is going on as if there was no war. The American people are going about their lives with little thought for what others have been asked to do in their name. This complaint is hardly new. But it seems more poignant to me when viewed through the prism of my Iraq experience. I do not mean to criticize Americans for going about their daily lives; they need to support their families and pursue their careers. No, I condemn the government for their success in making it so easy for everyone to forget the war and the crimes being committed in the name of the people.

Instead of asking for America's collective effort after 9/11, our elected leaders told us to just keep shopping, traveling, and driving—all of which results in guzzling gas, incidentally, which puts funds directly into the hands of terrorists. We were told to trust the government to defend us. All we needed to do, to keep America great and safe, was to consume—above all else, keep the dollars flowing. That is exactly what Americans obediently did. Cheap and easy credit made it possible to forget what was really happening. Thus, in rather quick fashion we were lulled into complacency soon after 9/11. Any who protested this response to the war were ignored at best, or were promptly and viciously vilified as unpatriotic, or even worse—as traitors. Remember the Dixie Chicks?

To be perfectly honest, that while I felt the same generalized "creeping malaise," as Pink Floyd would say, over the war, it wasn't until I received my recall notice that I was shocked back into reality. If you'll remember, I did not volunteer to go to Iraq. I was called back from the Individual Ready Reserve, into which I was placed while I waited for the processing of my resignation.

I opposed United States involvement in Iraq before it began and I oppose it to this day. I contrast my service with that of the lady's son from the Farmer's Market. He had volunteered for at least two extra tours in Iraq because he believed in what he was doing over there. To say the least, this very brief conversation greatly affected me. I still had to give that speech at the university and I realized that speaking with that lady had changed my perspective somewhat. My lack of support for the war didn't change, but my understanding of the lack of shared sacrifice had become broader and deeper. The speech that I had prepared was sorely unfit to unravel this concept before an audience, so I left the market and rewrote, as best I could, the main focus of my speech only hours before I was to give it.

During that first speech (the first public speech I had given since high school), I tried to impress upon my audience that Americans at home are not making any sacrifices while a small minority of us (those in the military and their families) are bearing the full burden of the war. During the formal Question and Answer period following, a bright young woman pointedly asked me how I could make such a bold claim when she felt that Americans are sacrificing their *civil liberties* for the war. My response was simple: I explained that liberty is not something we have the right to sacrifice. We sacrifice and die *for* liberty, we never surrender it. Yet that is exactly what we are doing: We are surrendering our liberties. After the event, the young woman and I engaged in a brief conversation. She explained the reasoning behind her question was an effort to "trip me up". However, instead of tripping me up, my answer turned the confusion back to her. She explained that my response made her aware that she had never thought of the difference between *surrender* and *sacrifice* in those terms before. She thanked me for my answer and told me that I had, in essence, given her something new to think about. Her question augmented my experience from the Farmer's Market. That question helped crystallize in my mind the theme of this book: Shared Sacrifice.

The interaction that I experienced with that speech gave me the unifying theme for my first attempt at mass communication. That young woman's question *directly* resulted in this book. That's proof of the power that Americans have when interacting with each other. However book reviewers might ultimately critique this work, that one hour session with an audience of about 100 college-age men and women sparked my creativity—and my passion. That's also proof of the power we have to influence each other. That's the power that created the strongest nation the world has ever seen. Sadly, these types of interactions are too few and far between. This lack of interaction, one American to another, allows fear to grow, which has placed our nation in the perilous state that we find ourselves today.

While the speech that resulted in the theme of this book was my first real public expression about the war, I have spoken with many people since. Some people seek me out because of my status as an Iraq war veteran, and others question me the moment they learn of it. In every conversation, I try to make the point that Americans are not sacrificing anything for what is *their* war. I have had very few people disagree with that notion. I had one person state, "What can I do? I'm a 5' blonde chick with no power. How can I make a difference?" It is encouraging that people are at least asking that question, even if in desperation. And desperation is what it will come to if we don't figure it out together.

The first thing to do is accept personal responsibility. I know that I had nothing to do with the decision to go to war in Iraq, and I have no power over the spinelessness of the elected "opposition" to it, but since I am a citizen of the United States, I am personally responsible for it. We all are. There's no escaping it—*you* are responsible. Some have chosen to respond to this responsibility by joining the military, or serving their country or community in other ways such as volunteer work. But the vast majority of people have responded to their responsibility by tuning out the crimes being committed in their name and doing just what the government expects of them: Continue shopping.

While the American public continues to casually shop, the military is deployed and overstretched in overseas combat operations in their name. People join the military for many different reasons: Some join for the job, some for education benefits, still others join out of family tradition. In the end, while their motivations to serve in the military can be classified into many discreet categories, ultimately, each person who joins does so for his or her own reasons. Nonetheless, they enter military service with the sworn intent to defend the Constitution of the United States of America, regardless of whether they personally joined to defend their homes, families, country, or personal liberty. Yes, these are some of the most common and important reasons why people join the military. Therefore, our young men and women who have died in Iraq have not died for Iraq, or the Iraqi people. Our soldiers have sacrificed their lives for *us and our continued liberties*—a fact which most Americans either don't know or forget.

This situation begs the question: While our soldiers are making sacrifices for us in Iraq and elsewhere around the world, what sacrifices are we making for our country, or for our troops? I'm sorry, but fading and neglected yellow ribbon magnets stuck to your car proclaiming your support for them just doesn't cut it. This situation requires action, not words. Words such as "weak on terror" have prevented much of what needs to be done to save our country's future; we have to stop fearing words and become angry at this inaction. And then we must turn our anger into resolve in order to make the sacrifices necessary for the preservation of our free and independent state.

When we accepted our Representatives' and Senators' votes to authorize the use of force in Iraq, we made a moral choice to go to war. Once that decision was made, we can have no other higher moral priority than fighting it smartly—with every available resource—and winning it as quickly as possible with the least possible suffering and loss of life. Once again, I ask: What are we, as a people, doing to ensure that this war is won and ended quickly? To listen to our elected "leaders" is to listen to the same worn out mantra of consumerism. They have told us to keep shopping—and driving—as if that alone will ensure victory. Is there anyone who actually believes that shopping will keep us free and protect us from terrorists? I realize that this question is absurd, but that is the nature of the very absurdity in which we find ourselves.

Even with the Army's well-publicized and chronic struggle to find enough people to fill recruitment quotas, I would never ask anyone not fully committed to join the military. Even with the obvious dire need for more people to make such a sacrifice, I would never encourage anyone with any reservations to serve. I understand that the prospect of violence is so abhorrent to some people that military service would never be an option for them. I respect that decision. However, military service is not the only way to serve our country. The first—and simplest—thing that we can do is to converse and interact with one another. I hope that some of us still remember the "old days" we see in Norman Rockwell paintings. You know, people laughing and talking on the front porch or sharing at a picnic. That's what our country needs: To become a community again.

In our 21st century "modern" world, our lives have become so full of distractions that we hardly have time to know ourselves, let alone our neighbors. I have heard so many people say exactly that: They don't know their neighbors. I freely admit that I am guilty of this also. We are all so preoccupied with our own little worlds that we fail to see other people that are literally within arms reach. In order to fight back against this separation from our communities—separation which facilitates the spread of fear—I have a small potential solution. My suggestion may seem a bit old fashioned (if not completely trite), but it can work. Here it is: Sugar. As in reenact that scene from so many sitcoms in American popular culture—where June Cleaver, Roseanne, or Will goes to the next door neighbor to borrow a cup of sugar. The purpose of the visit isn't because you actually need sugar, it is the interaction that takes place. Strike up a conversation with a stranger while you're waiting for the train. Help the little girl get her cat out of the tree. In short, get involved with your fellow Americans and be what Americans have always taken pride in being: Good neighbors. Don't wait. Put down this book for a minute and do it *now*.

I grant that these ideas are not new, and there is certainly no sacrifice in any of them, but charity and sacrifice are two sides of the same coin. If we can come together as a country again, we can—and *will* solve—every problem that arises, natural or man-made; and defeat any enemy, foreign or domestic. I know that we can do this. I have faith in myself as an American that I can do it, so I know that every American can. We're *supposed* to be the good guys. We *are* the good guys. It's time we start *acting* like it again.

*   *   *   *

In my interactions with audiences and colleagues regarding the topic of shared sacrifice, I have had only one person take genuine exception to my assertion that Americans as a whole are not sacrificing. I know that this person is not alone in his thinking, so I will abstract from it and say that "some people" have said that *paying taxes* is a sacrifice. Let me make this clear to anyone who believes that taxes are a sacrifice during war time: If you think that paying *money* is a sufficient sacrifice during war, you have no concept of sacrifice. Taxes are necessary for peace-time activities: Maintaining roads and bridges, regulating utilities, a functioning judiciary—*money* is not, and never has been, the price of liberty. Taxes are *not* a wartime sacrifice. If you believe that sacrifice during a national emergency amounts to only paying taxes, then you also have no concept of liberty—and you have never tasted war.

Taxes are something we pay to maintain our civilization—*profit* doesn't get the job done. The private sector, on its own, doesn't build or maintain roads for public use. Private companies do not pick up your garbage Monday mornings without profit. It takes collective resources—obtained through taxes—to build and maintain our roads and bridges, let alone maintain our national security (and if our bridges are any indication, we're not in very good shape on any front).

But even if we assume, for a very brief moment, that taxes do amount to a wartime sacrifice, the current overall level of taxation does not meet the requirements. Deficits are a tax on the future. Future generations will not only have to pay the nominal amount of the debt, but they will also have to contend with the ever-compounding interest, and compete in a global marketplace constrained with higher interest rates, and possibly staggering inflation. All of this means that the pain of the war—as measured in mere money—is just being put off to become the problem of future grandchildren of George W. Bush—if they ever had to actually pay a fair share of taxes.

We are unfairly burdening the upcoming generation of middle-class Americans with a problem of our creation. Given this inescapable responsibility we bear, it is our responsibility to take action and to do what we can with the time we have to fix it. It is *our* problem. Just because those currently in power refuse to do their duty, to lead sensibly and honestly, does not absolve us of our culpability in their malfeasance. We put them in power with our votes, and we will be the ones ultimately judged by history for their actions. It is our lack of oversight as a citizenry that has allowed this boondoggle on the future. How many of us have called or written our Representatives—regardless of their party affiliation—to tell them of our discontent over the war or demand oversight of the public's treasury? Have you written a letter? Expressed your concerns to your neighbors or coworkers? For the vast majority of us, the answer is "No". That is why, if the history of our time were to be written right now, it would be very unkind to us—and rightly so.

It is natural—and advisable—to run deficits during war time. And it is conceptually justifiable to put some of the expense of a war off to future generations (because we are betting on winning the war, and we will collectively pay the money back once we have won). In essence, deficits amount to us asking future generations to bear *some* of the burden. There is nothing inherently wrong with that. However, that is not what our "leaders" are doing. Right now our government has put off paying all financial obligations for this war. In fact, not one dime of taxation from current revenues has been spent on the wars in Iraq and Afghanistan. Every time the Bush Administration has claimed they need more money to fight the Global War on Terror, our Congress has acquiesced with few oversight committee hearings; what hearings that have been held were mere window dressing to give the appearance of debate. Congress has, without fail, submitted itself wholly to the will of the Administration and given money through borrowing and off-book financing that is not included in the regular budget. This is another Enron waiting to happen on a *continental* scale, and it will leave none of us unscathed.

Not once, or so it would seem from the drunken-sailor like spending spree this war has been, have any of our leaders asked the really hard, yet most obvious question: Where is this money coming from? By not asking this question they have allowed everyone, especially themselves, the luxury of looking good. This in turn allows them to claim, "See we're keeping spending under control, the *budget* deficit is so small!" Unfortunately, in order to believe that, you have to forget the hundreds of billions they have borrowed—in our name—to maintain that charade. One thing they desperately need you to forget is this: Politicians overwhelmingly fall within the upper tax brackets receiving the largest share of recent tax breaks—so they won't be paying for any of this even when the bills finally do start coming due. These are mere politicians, not a leader among them. This may sound overly bitter, and perhaps it is, but these are the people who sent our nation to war without giving any thought to the purpose of the war, how to pay for it or even how to end it.

Where is the sharing of the sacrifice in any of this? Why are the wealthiest people among us—those who derive most of their income from passive sources such as rent and dividends—not asked to share any of the cost, let alone the sacrifice? If we are truly a united people, we are supposed to be in this together. In reality, it seems that only the ever-shrinking middle class and the increasing ranks of the poor are the ones asked to make any sacrifice, whether voluntarily or not. While many volunteer for military service because of economic circumstance, military service is not the only way the middle class and poor are presently, or *will* pay, for our war. I say "will pay" for the war because we're not doing it yet. The government will eventually (probably sooner rather than later) be forced to make hard choices. Given their phobia of taxation on those most able to bear the financial burden, the result will be budget cut-backs in necessary services such as police, health care, education, and transportation—all of which will directly affect the vast majority of regular Americans. A sad portent indeed, and when this happens, there will be no one to blame but ourselves. Our share of the sacrifice will be *forced* upon us by unforgiving circumstance.

It has been my personal experience—as I'm sure it has been the experience of every adult—that it is better to pay as you go along. Putting off pain only compounds it when it finally arrives. We should not be asking generations yet to be born to shoulder a burden that we are creating and refusing to carry ourselves. Most of us have learned this the hard way, through the overuse of borrowing through easy but expensive credit. Like the vast majority of Americans, I have fallen into this trap myself. Now we collectively face severe financial problems because our government can't wean itself from the borrowing spigot. This pain will touch everyone. And its root cause is that we do not demand that our politicians do other than they have been doing. It is our fault.

One of the worst things about all of this is that those who are actually *profiting* from the war are asked to make no sacrifices at all. In the name of the "free market", our government time and again grants huge lopsided tax breaks—or just hands large sums of our money directly—to corporations. Corporations are in the marketplace to make profit. If they are inefficient, they should lose, that's the name of the game. But it is interesting to note that our elected adherents to the marketplace endlessly work to provide loopholes to large, inefficient corporations for no other reason than to keep them in business and to ensure their profits. Big corporations, whose management professes belief in the power of the "free market" to efficiently allocate resources, are always the first to push their snouts into the public trough of unjustifiable government largesse. And the government has proven more than eager to please. If these corporations were worth their share prices, they wouldn't need corporate welfare, on the backs, and at the expense of the American taxpayer. But there we are: A government defined and defended by cronies.

The Farmer's Market of yesteryear has given way to the impersonal commerce of international trade, at great expense to us as a country. And the expense cannot only be expressed in terms of dollars. Can you remember a few years ago when Wal-Mart, our country's dominant retailer, used to proudly proclaim that their merchandise was mostly made in the USA? I only use Wal-Mart as an example, because it is certainly not alone in this. But it makes me wonder: When did becoming a low-cost competitor become more important than being a patriotic American company committed to American jobs and community?

Don't get me wrong, I'm not a communist. I actually happen to believe in the fundamentals of the marketplace, but I also believe that we owe something to each other, as a country, a nation, and a people, beyond mere goods and services. We owe each other a government that will make a good faith attempt to keep us safe from those that seek to do us harm. We owe each other a country with a functioning marketplace in which we can each live our lives in peace, find our individual callings, care for our families, and make our livings. America is much more than just a marketplace in which the no-holds-barred profit-making of old rules.

As we consider this fact, it is vitally important that we realize that our individual liberties do not boil down to mere economic wellbeing. America has always been the land of opportunity. Sadly, for some, opportunity equates only with profit. But for many others, like me, opportunity has different meanings. For some people, opportunity means being able to follow your personal dreams, whatever they may be, regardless of money. Of course, everyone needs to make a living and in America, when the rules are consistent and fair for everyone, a good living (and even profit) can be made. But the rules being set by our politicians are ever increasingly at odds with the notion of fairness. Legislation is always being considered (and passed) to hold individuals increasingly accountable for their economic behavior while at the same time shielding corporations from their misbehavior.

Two recent congressional actions illustrate this starkly and well. On the one hand, bankruptcy laws have become ever tighter, making it more difficult than ever before for desperately indebted Americans to receive a fresh start. At the same time, Congress has allowed the Superfund Law—a law responsible for cleaning up much of the environmental disasters resulting from small-minded corporate profit-taking—to become de-funded by allowing the taxes on the industries most responsible for the pollution to lapse[1]. Why are corporations, as a class (of artificial person) given special rights and protections at the expense of flesh and blood Americans? Is corporate greed a rallying cry worthy of the sacrifice in blood of American servicemen and women?

Why is it that Congress, enabled by the Administration, will pass legislation every chance they get to keep Americans from taking care of each other through social programs? This directly results in keeping individual Americans—and American families—on the verge of economic disaster. Look no further than the 2007 veto by President Bush of the popular, and desperately needed, State Children's Health Insurance Program (SCHIP) expansion—a veto which was upheld by his GOP cronies in Congress. While they are denying Americans the opportunity to collectively care for one another, they are refusing, for even a moment, to second-guess spending tens of billions of dollars a year on yet more unproven weapons technologies. They claim that the technology, in the form of advanced weapons systems, is needed to protect us against threats that either are too secret to tell us about (if you are that generous) or don't exist. You can bet that actually gaining *protections* from these theoretical weapons systems (which often take decades to design and test—and result in failures) has nothing to do with their funding—it has to do with ensuring profit for campaign contributors. Where can one find in our implied social contract with each other that corporate greed should be the unifying theme of our government's policies and actions?

There are as many for-profit contractors in Iraq today as there are American servicemen and women. Halliburton, KBR, and Blackwater are probably the most famous (or infamous), but they are certainly not the only ones. In supplanting public need for private profit through the outsourcing of traditional governmental duties such as national defense, our government has betrayed its primary function—to provide for the common defense, promote the general welfare and secure the blessings of liberty.

Our government's fanatical zeal for the free market and private corporations has removed the necessary collective sacrifice from our national defense. Continually outsourcing military functions, right down to "kitchen patrol", has moved us into a world of corporate integration at every level and function of our government. This leads us to the crisis we now face: The prospect of tyranny. Private contractors doing the work of police here at home is not too far down the road. Let me say that again: Private contractors—acting as a *private police force*—enforcing our laws is a real possibility. We already had a taste of that when Blackwater was busy in New Orleans in the aftermath of Hurricane Katrina. Such duties are the responsibility of those charged with guarding our nation. Perhaps we should consider some sort of "National Guard"? Oh, I forgot we have one, but it and its equipment are too busy guarding another nation: Iraq.

We must engage the government now and force them to change—before it's too late. Congress has proven to be so cowardly that they cannot even protect our Constitution from a cabal of self-serving profiteers exploiting fear. Although they should be—and will be—held accountable for their treachery, it is We the People who are really to blame, and we will rightly pay the price for our lack of vigilance. We have allowed them to lie to and steal from us for generations. It's been going on so long now that we have become accustomed to it. And because of this, we have become a complacent people, burdened with an ever increasing fascination of the most recent celebrity foible, when the burden of keeping an eternally vigilant eye on our government is our ultimate responsibility.

If you expect elected representatives to look out for your well-being, you need to take a hard look at who you vote for. Are those currently seated doing what needs to be done to maintain our national security, provide for the common welfare, and protect our fundamental liberties, or are they choosing to disregard liberty for security, knowing that by so doing they cannot guarantee either?

While much of what I have said thus far may seem to be about us, we in fact owe nothing to ourselves. We owe everything to those who will come after us. Look at it this way, if the founders of our country had been selfish and cared only about their generation, and their land and wealth—such as our "leaders" do today—they would have found an accommodation with King George III. They would have sought preferential treatment and betrayed their countrymen for their personal short-term well-being. The same choice faces us today, only this time our "leaders" have chosen to make that accommodation. They have chosen to partner with corporations to sell out the American dream in exchange for campaign contributions. I'm not telling you anything you don't already know.

Our founders stood up, in the name of the people, to the government of their time. They knowingly and willingly risked their lives, fortunes and sacred honor. They had the foresight to take these risks not only for themselves, but for their posterity—for us. Who are we to fail to carry on their work? If they were willing to stand up and say, "No more!" Who are we to abandon those who will come after us to a fate of tyranny and possible slavery? It has happened before—right here on these shores—and it can happen again.

As I have reflected on my short time on this planet, I have come to the stark realization that if I were to die today, I would leave the world worse off than I found it. Why? The answer is simple—I was silent in the face of such peril. I can no longer afford that luxury. As I write this, I know that I am making a difference. If even one person reads this book and steps up to make a change, I will consider this a success. But in order for that to happen, I must be an example. This book is my *first* example. I have sacrificed so little to try to make the world a better place. But what little I have suffered now makes me stronger—and able to shout from the rooftops to be heard; to try to gain the assistance of my fellow Americans in a wave of much needed change. I feel like I am a lonely voice in the wilderness, but I'm sure *someone* will hear me.

I am not so naïve to believe that sacrifice for America means mere writing or speaking. I understand that words are the necessary starting point. However, we must use the right words, words that seek out action—and inspire us. Our words must not be a simple litany of complaints. I have noticed that those in opposition to the way our government is conducting our affairs talk and write a great deal, but that hasn't led to much popular action. Sure, there have been large street protests, but what has that really accomplished? The government has ignored us at every turn. If we are going to make meaningful change, we need to examine who we are as a people, through an evaluation of the actions we take and solutions we pose with our words.

This examination begins with this simple question: What is America about? A cursory glance at our consumption-driven society would indicate that, in many respects, America has become just a (dangerously unsecured) physical border with commodities inside to be bought and sold—a continent-sized strip mall. This is not America to me. America is an idea. It is not just made up of omnipresent shopping centers, packed with big-box stores, polluted by gas-guzzling SUV's, and surrounded by miles of freeways.

No, America is not about consumerism. It is about the freedom to act, associate and speak as we see fit, with very limited government intrusion in our lives. The question then becomes: Is America worth dying for or just worth living in? That is what it comes down to. You need to ask yourself that question. Death is the ultimate price, and if you come to the conclusion that America is worth dying for, then protecting it for those who come after us is worth risking everything: Life, fortune, and sacred honor, just like our forefathers. Allow me to reach back to the mid-1980's for a convenient pop culture reference, thanks to Phil Collins. Our country is not worth dying for if it's not a "place worth living in." Our country will not be worth living in if we destroy the very things that make it America—such as our precious and hard-won liberties.

We were taught, in public schools for many of us, that our Republic was founded on bedrock philosophies which have been enshrined in our Constitution. Certain inviolate freedoms, protections from government intrusion, and a balance of governmental authority, are at the center of our rule of law. We stand today on the cusp of losing many of the fundamental protections of that rule of law in the name of defeating an enemy whose main purpose is to do *just that*: To destroy the principles that make America the strongest country on Earth.

I talk about these liberties a great deal. So much so that some would say I'm a broken record (for those of you who have never actually heard a damaged vinyl record, just think of me as a scratched CD that keeps skipping and playing the same snippet of song over and over again). Our liberties, and the principles upon which they are based, constitute the philosophical backbone of our civilization. Allow me to make a quick suggestion for those of you who doubt me, take about

30 minutes, Google up the National Archives, and *read the U.S. Constitution*! Oh, and while you're at it, take a look at the Declaration of Independence as well. Oh hell, screw it! I've put a copy of both in the Appendices for your reading convenience.

Back to my original point: Since it is undeniable that our liberties are the foundation of our society, it therefore flies in the face of logic to believe that we can win the battle with fundamentalist zealots by betraying the principles that have kept us free and independent for more than two hundred years. To surrender any of our principles, even temporarily in the name of national security, is to *admit the absolute defeat of those principles.*

However, our "leaders" did just that: They surrendered our liberties, in the face of fear, with the limp excuse of "keeping us safe". By passing the Military Commissions Act of 2006 and signing it into law, Congress and the president gave *considerable aid and comfort to our enemies* by handing them a victory they could never have achieved by force. This Act codified the erosion of the most fundamental protection in our Constitution—the writ of habeas corpus[2]. This writ guarantees you the right to challenge your detention by the government in a court of law. I will discuss this in some detail in a later chapter, but it is important for you to understand now that *without this right, all other rights become unenforceable.*

If we are in a life-and-death struggle for the future of American values, how can our representatives explain subjugating our central traditions to petty political expediency? Because we live in a form of representative democracy, we, as a people, are responsible and must answer for the mistakes of our elected representatives. We must accept this responsibility; otherwise we must stand at History's bar and explain our *shame* to the countless thousands of men and women who have given their lives throughout history for the ideals of our country. All because Congress has taken the steps to destroy the very ideals for which our brothers and sisters sacrificed—all because of fear.

It is important to recognize that the only real weapon possessed by terrorists is fear. And it is apparently very effective, if you measure our government's response to it. Their obvious surrender to fear is a victory for those who wish to destroy the American way of life. Do you find it reasonable to live in fear? As individuals, we can each wake up one morning and refuse to live in fear any longer. But when will we come together to refuse to live in fear as a country? It takes strength and leadership to do that. I know we have the strength, but where is the leadership?

Right now it seems that our leadership is more interested in using fear as a weapon *against us*. Every time there has been serious opposition to some plan to usurp another of your freedoms, some bureaucrat would come on TV and announce some new threat to your safety. And the opposition obediently would melt away, just because of an unproven assertion of some undefined threat—a threat which later turns out to never have existed in the first place. That's the unmistakable trait of the leadership we have today: When faced with opposition, use and surrender to fear.

But this fact has been long missing from the debate: Leadership through fear and secrecy is not leadership, it is cowardice. A government that does not trust the people to do what is right is not worthy of the people's trust. To say that one person (or even a whole government) should have the authority to seize any person and hold him or her without charge, and without access to the courts, based merely on open-ended suspicion, is the very essence of the tyranny our founders despised. But today we actually have laws that allow this to happen. How we treat those accused of a crime says less about the alleged transgressor than about who we are as a people. Once again, the question must be asked: Is our nation ruled by fear? I, for one, refuse to live afraid of cowardly terrorists. And I equally refuse to surrender one ounce of liberty to my government for the mere appearance of security I know they can never guarantee.

Again, while we must hold our elected representatives accountable for their crimes of capitulation, we cannot forget who is ultimately responsible: We are. So many people are willing to idly stand by and surrender their liberty while American servicemen and women are literally dying for that same liberty halfway around the world. We should be ashamed of ourselves for allowing corrupt politicians to betray not only our principles, but also our troops.

Yet we hear so much about how our politicians support those troops. They wrap themselves in the flag every chance they get and proclaim grand words of allegiance to our principles, but when it comes time for actual action they can't run away from those principles fast enough. I am personally sickened by these fawning parasites. When asked who my congressman is I answer I don't have one—no one in Congress represents me. This person is not re-elected every two years, he's re-anointed, and represents only what his corporate sponsors tell him to represent. These are not real men and women of strength and conviction, they are toadies.

And presidents are not meant to *make* friends, the job naturally requires that they *lose* them. So why does President Bush have so many stalwart friends? The answer is simple: Profit. So many cronies are beholden to him for their place at the Treasury's trough that they will never back away from support for him and his war of choice. Our money: Feeding cronies. Do you believe that people who would betray our principles for profit would make the necessary sacrifices to preserve our Constitution?

*   *   *   *

It is time to wake up, America! It is time to recognize that in order to win not just in the Global War on Terror, but also win the war to save our Republic, we must be prepared to take great risks. Yes, there are things worth fighting for, and such fights often mean risking death. Life is literally worthless if we have nothing greater than our own small lives. Surrendering liberty, even to our own government, is against our nature as Americans, and those in Washington must be constantly reminded that they will not escape our wrath—at the polls and in courts of justice. Their betrayal *will* be punished. There is only one thing our politicians should fear, and it isn't the people in the opposing political party: It is We the People retaking the government from the stranglehold of their two corrupt political parties.

As one of our greatest patriots, Nathan Hale, famously said before being executed in 1776 by the British, "I only regret that I have but one life to lose for my country."[3] He did not say, "I only regret that I have but one life to lose for profit". Is there anyone reading this book who doubts that our "leaders" today are more interested in money and personal power than principles, lives, and freedoms?

Remember the old saying that "The price of liberty is eternal vigilance". We cannot relent in our offensive against our enemies and this requires that we remain ever vigilant against those in our own government who would seek to destroy our system in the name of saving it. Our principles and the underlying philosophy on which they are based make us who were are. If we proclaim these fundamental principles to be "quaint", we betray our predecessors, our descendants, and ourselves.

The less secure your civil liberties, the less secure your actual security. The government has an increasing disincentive to protect you physically when they are not compelled to respect your liberty. If we keep turning a collective blind eye to these disgraceful and illegal powers being seized wholesale by our government, no individual can expect anyone else to notice or act when it is he that is taken in the dead of night.

Protecting ourselves from government intrusion is just as important as protecting ourselves against foreign threats. Patriotism requires that we remain true to our core principles. It takes a great deal more than wrapping oneself in a flag and spouting empty rhetoric to be a patriot. It requires an actual *willingness* to sacrifice, and this willingness can only be demonstrated through action.

I would hope that everyone reading this is a true patriot, and as such accepts that a patriot not only sacrifices for liberty, but is prepared to die for liberty. We can never compromise on that. As I pointed out earlier, right now we Americans are not sacrificing our liberties, we are surrendering them without a fight. Happily, there appears to be some noticeable groundswell against the government's overreach. But Congress doesn't seem to notice or care what we think. They do what they are told by their corporate masters. It is never too late to regain the liberties we have already lost, but while we are engaged in that fight, we have to keep a close eye on our government and constantly guard against further encroachment.

Our soldiers are fighting in Iraq. Our soldiers are fighting in Afghanistan. Our soldiers fight everyday for liberty, all around the world. Yet when they come home, they find fewer liberties than when they left. It takes more than money and words to support the troops. It takes a tireless commitment to our principles and our rule of law. Right now, our troops are not being supported by our government. We have a cowardly Congress betraying the people in general and specifically the soldiers in the name of "balancing liberty with security" (which in the parlance of politicians is code for "fear"). But they forget that *liberty is security.*

However, we have to keep in mind that we are a self-governed Republic. Right or wrong, our government speaks and acts in our name. Their crimes are *our* crimes. And their lack of resolve in the face of fear is our failing. Why is there no integrity left in our government? Why must we keep electing opportunists? It doesn't feel as if We the People are part of the government any longer. Because of this, our government has rightfully lost all legitimacy. We must take back our country by electing people who understand that we live in a world of danger, but who equally understand that no threat of danger is worth the loss of *any* fundamental liberty. As Nathan Hale proudly and valiantly demonstrated, *America is worth dying for.*

It has been said of Americans that the things that unite us are greater than the things that divide us. It is nice to believe that, but looking at America today, I'm not so sure that's accurate. I want to believe that we can regain that, but it will take effort—from all of us. Right now, though, Americans are increasingly intolerant of differing points of view, just like that lady at the Farmer's Market in Laramie. I don't blame her for not coming to an event that was billed as an "Iraq War Veteran Speaks Against The War", but if she had come, she could have engaged me in a debate. She could have stood up and made points of her own—

in front of an audience willing to listen. I wish she had come. Americans need each other if we are to overcome our enemies.

But we tend to consume only news and entertainment that contains a slant—conservative or liberal—that reinforces what we already "know". We don't seriously listen to those we disagree with. This is a weakness. It is time for us to get out of that comfort zone, and to engage the opposition. None of us alone has all the correct answers and we will only find them if we discover them by working *together*.

*   *   *   *

As I have said before, I would not encourage anyone to join the military. I believe that requires such a commitment that can only come from the heart. A person should not be forced or manipulated into putting on a uniform, but if they are called by their heart, friends and families should support that. We need young men and women who want to sacrifice—the lure of adventure is always strong for the young—and we should encourage that, in whatever form it takes. And we should not artificially restrict those who want to serve just because of some policy based upon a contrived sense of morality. There are Americans who wish to serve their country in uniform, openly and honestly, true to who they are as human beings, but our government has barred them from doing so for no other reason than their sexual orientation. Imagine it: At a time of national emergency when sharing the sacrifice is essential, some willing, talented, and able Americans are being turned away from our collective fight for freedom.

This brings me to the concept of proportional sacrifice. We are a strong enough country to literally have both guns and butter, but not in unlimited amounts; a line must be drawn somewhere and priorities made. At some point, decisions—hard decisions—have to be made and our government today is afraid of making them. They want to give us the constant illusion that we can have it all—everything at the same time. As ludicrous as it is on its face, our government has lulled many Americans into believing their doublespeak which proclaims that we can have peace and war at the same time. Think about it: You see war on the TV every night when you're eating dinner, and yet when the news is over, you go about watching the sitcoms—the war never really touches you, does it? So, during that half hour each day, you see the war that our brave soldiers are fighting, but the rest of the time you concern yourself with the details of your life. I'm not blaming anyone who this describes; I have fallen into this trap myself.

As long as we remember that *every* American has responsibility for what our government does—and fails to do—we will retain the power to extract ourselves from this situation. But if we forget that simple truth and keep living as we have in the dark, it will get darker. It will be a much harder fight to regain what we are losing once it is lost. And we will bestow that hard fight to future generations. There is no honor in that.

Like the vendors at a Farmer's Market, we each have something to provide to America. We all have some skin in this game. We can all flourish together in comfort with liberty or we can languish together in poverty and fear. But prosperity doesn't come without risk. There are sacrifices we must each make. If you are young and able, you need to step up and use your energy to better the community around you. If you are older and less agile, you need to share your wisdom. We all have something to offer—right up until we die—to this great country. We owe it to each other and to the future to fight *now* before it's too late.

I have lamented in these pages how Americans, as individuals, have very little at risk with regard to the sacrifices being made in the Global War on Terror. There are certainly those who have paid the ultimate price—and we must not forget them or their families—but generally, most Americans have little personal stake in what is happening. I have also outlined how we are surrendering our liberties through complacency. But in the interest of being fair and balanced, I want to turn to what sacrifices we *are* collectively making and what costs we are paying for the Global War on Terror.

We are losing—if we have not already lost—our national honor. Our government claims that it does not torture, but as of this writing, many new revelations about the Administration's secret interrogation programs are coming to light. For years, the Bush Administration has stated in public that "The United States doesn't torture", while at the same time relying on secret memos written by lawyers (not authorized by any *actual law*, mind you, they were mere *opinion memos* written by *lawyers*), redefining torture so that the actual torture methods employed by the U.S. government no longer fall within the treaty-created definition of the word "torture". Water-boarding, a technique universally defined as torture since the Inquisition, is now redefined, in the 21st Century, as "enhanced interrogation"[4]. Unbelievable. Shameful. Illegal.

America, that beacon of hope, is becoming a pariah amongst civilized nations. And, from what I've seen, and given that we let these criminals continue to run our country, such judgment from our traditional allies is not unwarranted. We are a people governed by men and women with hearts full of fear and we have allowed them to torture people in our name. We cannot claim ignorance. Ignorance is not a defense when a self-governed Republic betrays the principles on which it was founded and denies the rule of law.

You will not be shocked when I tell you that I have heard some people argue that the United States of America *should be allowed* to torture terrorist suspects. These people state, without any sense of irony whatsoever, that "terrorists would do it to us". Such arguments fail to take into account an important point: We are *different* from our enemies. If we start acting like them, we have nothing left to fight for. Adopting our enemies' methods would be a tacit surrender to their ideals. Do we want to become like them?

Using the methods employed by our enemies also weakens us. It forces us to lose sight of who we are and what we're about. Our allies from other nations have traditionally looked to us for leadership. Not just economic leadership, but *moral* leadership. In allowing our government to betray our principles, we have not only betrayed ourselves, we have betrayed the trust others around the world have shown. They used to turn to us as a model of goodness and decency. Not any more.

That moral high-ground that we once occupied, gave us an aura of invincibility in the face of our enemies. It could be forcefully and justifiably argued that that aura *by itself* prevented wars. Our collective strength of purpose and moral resolve to do what was right could not be compromised. But we can no longer claim that. Our government has turned that hopeful aura of white light into a sickly green pallor of shame.

Right now, more than we have ever needed before, we need people to stand up to their own government. It will take more than a generation to clean up this mess, but we have overcome greater obstacles. We have come together to throw off tyranny cloaking other people. We have endured hardship for what we knew was right. We can—and must—do it again. For our own sake and the sakes of those that come after.

*   *   *   *

The American experiment in self-governance has always been about self-betterment. We expanded our country through exploration and settlement. We tamed our vast wilderness and built the strongest country in history. We developed the most advanced public education system in the world and we have been pioneers in man's reach for the stars. To transport our goods, we designed and built roads across the country so we can all share in the bounty of this land. We can therefore conclude that the greatest resource America has always depended on is that of our people. Sharing in each other's triumphs and helping mitigate each other's misfortune. Being a community of people—not just business interests—is what made America great. I fear we are losing that community. But that community is exactly the tool we will need to turn to in order to retain (or would it be more accurate to say regain?) our greatness.

Americans are smart, strong, and willing to sacrifice. There are literally countless stories of individual Americans' bravery and charity—I believe *every* American has such stories to tell about him or herself. We have proof from struggles past of our collective willingness to sacrifice. What is different now? The answer is our government doesn't want us to sacrifice. They believe that if they ask us to sacrifice they will lose our support—not understanding our sincere desire to do what is right regardless of the cost. Our "leaders" do not understand the American character. Our own politicians are selling *us* short, out of fear of hurting *their* image. It is sickening. For them, high office is an end in itself; they forget that high office is meant to be high service.

It is time for some *true* American patriots to stand up and seek those offices. Americans concerned about the state of our country and the course we are taking. We need Americans who know that America is a country founded on sacrifice and that our collective sacrifice is the direct cause of our collective prosperity. That prosperity is quickly slipping from our grasp, but we can hold on if enough of us step up to the challenge and go to work. Your country needs you! *Now!*

FEAR

The main point I was trying to make in the Farmer's Market chapter was that America is a community. That community stretches from our immediate neighborhood to our city, to our state and ultimately includes our entire country. Without the community, we are left alone to protect ourselves from malevolent harm. Yes, there are some of us who are so confident in our own abilities to defend ourselves that we feel we do not need others for help. To those I say, "Fine. It's your right to take your fate into your own hands." But what about those less skilled or fit to do that, people such as your parents or children? Can you protect *them* at all times? The answer is undoubtedly, "No".

Most of us do not feel that we can adequately—and constantly—protect ourselves from crime or disaster. So we turn to the community and band together to provide protection to each other. It is natural that we do this. Our individual civil liberties are a direct extension of the protection we provide to each other. In fact, in our system, our civil liberties are the *basis* of our collective security.

In order to effectively provide protections to each other through the mechanisms of the community, we entrust power to a few people to oversee those efforts. In our method of self-governance, we knowingly and by design withheld certain authorities from government officials, with the intent and result that our civil liberties were created and forcefully protected.

But one of the powers that our system does grant to those officials is the authority to declare and wage war in our name. This authority is required and fundamental for our national defense. Naturally, we expect those responsible to wage wars in a deliberate manner, with the intent of winning as quickly as possible with as little suffering as possible—on all sides. One war which has been thrust upon us is the so-called Global War on Terror. It is a bumper sticker slogan, I know, but I use it because it encompasses both the good and bad of how we are trying to defend ourselves.

Our government has made the conscious decision to use fear in fighting the Global War on Terror. Fear is a valid weapon when employed against the enemy. It can lead the enemy to lay down his arms to avoid further death and destruction, as evidenced by the Japanese surrender in World War II (don't take that as an implicit endorsement of using atomic weapons, I am merely pointing out that the Japanese government made the rational decision to surrender in order to avoid further mass destruction—a decision reached through the use of fear).

Those currently in our nation's leadership positions have made no secret of their desire for Americans to be afraid. In fact, they *need* us to be afraid of random violence, injury, or death. They need us to fear these things so that we will not question when they grab the power to do as they please in the fight against terrorism. But everyday it becomes more apparent that they are exploiting that fear in order to maintain and increase their power over *us*, both individually and collectively. And we have fallen for their ruse. We accept their danger-around-every-corner claims and give them whatever power they say they need in order to keep us safe. Please note that this is an unmistakable manifestation of *our surrender to fear*.

But we haven't surrendered everything yet, we still have the rule of law, right? Not so much. Those in government increasingly believe that they no longer have to abide by the limits we have placed on their power. Because of this, our community is weakened and we are individually placed at great risk. That risk is intensified by our lack of regular interaction with our neighbors. It is not far fetched to believe that you, a U.S. citizen, could be taken by government agents, interrogated harshly (read: *tortured*) until you confess to whatever it is they want you to confess to, and then held in isolation without charge for years and without access to the courts. No, this is not far fetched at all. It has happened already, and not in the distant past; it happened just a few years ago in a well-publicized case. And as far as we know, this is not the only case of this type of treatment at the hands of an out-of-control, unaccountable, and increasingly criminal government. It is likely to be happening to many other U.S. citizens that we don't know about. This treatment is most definitely happening to non-U.S. citizens in secret "black site" prisons around the world.

It is vital that we keep in mind—always—that these things are being done in our name and with our consent. As long as we fail to hold those responsible accountable to us—and to history—we have consented to this. We have only ourselves to blame. How could this happen? We were the moral leaders of the world during the Cold War because of our unwavering adherence to the principles of liberty and judicial fairness. How could we allow fear to take over and permit ourselves to become a pariah amongst the civilized countries of the world?

I believe I have an answer to that question: Within the first few weeks of arriving at Iraq, I had the chance to have lunch with one of my unit's sergeants. We were talking about the Global War on Terror—which was a topic I would revisit many times with many different people throughout my tour. The person I was eating with believed that the government should be able to take anyone off the streets anytime they like if they believe them to be a terrorist suspect. This brought to my mind the so-called "dirty bomber", Jose Padilla.

He is an American citizen, taken on American soil and he was held without charge or access to counsel because the government chose to label him "Enemy Combatant". I pointed this out to my colleague, who believed that was no big deal. After going around and around with him for about 20 minutes on this, he finally said, "You *know* that he had to have done *something* wrong". My friend here had fallen into the government's trap: If the government accuses, there must be guilt.

"Fine," I said, "Then why doesn't the government prove it in a court of law? Let's say that I claim you have committed a crime, I have no evidence that can be presented in court, but I claim it anyway and take you away. I deny you access to a lawyer and access to the courts because to let you defend yourself in a court of law could hurt "national security"—my words merely claiming it makes it so. How would you feel about that? Should the government be able to seize you anywhere and hold you without charge because they *can't* prove your guilt?" In the end, I don't believe I won him over because he seemed to still believe that the government would never take someone off the street and hold them without charge for no good reason. I wondered to myself which one of us was the actual idealist.

Sadly, it seems, there are so many Americans who feel as my colleague did. But for those people reading this book that feel this way, I give you this warning: Don't give a president that you trust power you don't want future presidents—whom you *won't* trust—to have. I am far more suspicious of my government. And that is how the framers wanted it: That healthy suspicion is actually written into the U.S. Constitution that I swore to uphold. We have a system of checks and balances whereby three separate but equal branches of government have oversight of one another—they balance each other through the checks they have on each other's power. I'm not telling you something you don't already know. I am just trying to remind you of what we Americans are actually fighting for.

I want to emphasize a point I tried to make to my fellow soldier: Our government has taken an American citizen (at least one we know of for sure) and held him without charge or access to the courts because they *couldn't prove his guilt*. They held him until they could develop a case on which he could be convicted. Think about that. Whatever your feelings are about the specifics of the Padilla case, this is what happened: An American citizen was taken on American soil, held for years without charge or access to a lawyer and then not even tried for the crime for which he was originally arrested. This isn't like the OJ Simpson case where public opinion believes him guilty, but he was acquitted. No, this is a case where the government didn't even have enough evidence to *file charges*, let alone convict on the original suspicion. Yet they held him for years.

Imagine *you* being held in similar circumstances. Arrested for something you didn't do and held until the government had enough time to *create* a case against you—any case at all that will provide them with a much-needed conviction. Justice has nothing whatsoever to do with this, it is theatre designed to demonstrate success in the Global War on Terror.

You should always keep in mind that our system of criminal justice is based on a presumption of innocence. Put yourself in this place: You are now the "defendant", and the government has no evidence with which to convict you for the crime you were originally arrested. Even if you have evidence to prove your innocence, the government will not allow you access to a lawyer to make the arguments and present the evidence in a court, nor will it allow you even access to the court itself—for no other reason than their claim of "national security" (which is undoubtedly just code for, "We don't have the proof required to convict you.")

I am not a legal scholar, but I have studied comparative political theory and American civics. Our system was once very strong because those in government had a true sense of right and wrong. They may have been self-aggrandizing, as most politicians will be at times, but they stood firm—and together—against our enemies. Regardless of their levels of fear, they protected the Constitution and upheld the checks and balances created by it. Why is our level of commitment to due process so shattered by the fear created by cowardly conspiratorial terrorists? How is it that our government can allow a handful of criminal zealots to bring down our way of life just by bringing down the Twin Towers?

To help keep your mind in full gear, imagine that someone—again, let's say *you*—comes to the interest of the National Security Agency, Central Intelligence Agency, Federal Bureau of Investigation or some other "intelligence" bureaucracy within the U.S. government because someone has stolen your wallet and is using your identity for criminal purposes. Your name is put on some "watch list", and as you arrive at an airport to go on vacation, you are seized and labeled an unlawful enemy combatant—a terrorist. You are detained and denied access to a lawyer. No one believes anything you say because everyone knows that a suspected terrorist would say anything. And if you keep asking for that lawyer you're "entitled to", well, that just proves you must be a terrorist—because it is their view that only a criminal would ask for a lawyer. You don't believe this can happen? Just wait, if things keep going as they have recently, it will be far too familiar an experience for many Americans—and their families.

This leads to the question: How does someone come to the attention of the government? Well, that's easy. Just exercise your rights and they will notice. Take part in a public protest, or check out a controversial book from the library which condemns the government's overreach, and you can become interesting to them. And they will do "whatever it takes" to determine how much of a threat you are. Their methods begin, but certainly don't end, with warrantless wiretaps.

✳   ✳   ✳   ✳

I don't want to walk onto the set of a bad conspiracy movie or anything, but has anyone given any thought to the fact that warrantless searches and eavesdropping could lead to government officials *planting* evidence and then charging people with "regular" crimes to silence opposition? The slow steady erosion of the fundamental liberties necessary to maintaining a functioning democracy are under assault with these and other efforts designed to "make us safe". Apparently our liberties themselves are also a threat and we need protection from them, if you are to follow the government's line of reasoning.

However, the situation is even more chilling than it appears. The very foundational right that underpins all others has already come under sustained attack. What about when the government charges you or a member of your family with evidence that they tell the judge you shouldn't be able to see? This is *secret* evidence that you can't see, so your lawyer can't argue against it—if they let you have a lawyer, that is. But you don't really need a lawyer: You're guilty—trust us. Sound crazy? Well, unfortunately, it's far from crazy—it's the direction in which we are headed. Due to a little bit of legislation known as the Military Commissions Act of 2006, the key right to all the others, *habeas corpus*, has already suffered a near fatal blow.

Why is this right, and the passage of this Act, so important? To answer the first, it is vital to understand that the ultimate act of state violence is to hold a person without an opportunity to challenge the authority of the state to imprison the individual. This right was first created in the Magna Carta almost 800 years ago in England. This concept was so important when it was created that the English *nobility* rose up in their own revolution against their king to *force* its creation. Imagine that. To give this some perspective, you can think of the English nobility of that time as being the same as our profit-driven corporations of today. Imagine *them* rising against the government that gives them no-bid contracts, corporate welfare, and unreasonably low taxes, and you get the idea of how significant this right really is.

When—not if—your government imprisons you for exercising your right of religion or speech, for example, the key to your defense against further state violence is the ability to go to a court and demand that the state produce charges or a justification to warrant your imprisonment. Therefore, because all rights rely on the ability of the individual to challenge the authority of the state when they are violated, by eroding the right of habeas corpus the state effectively begins the inevitable erosion of *all* other rights.

Some might say that the Military Commissions Act only applies to non-U.S. citizens. Be that as it may, it is nonetheless the first step in destroying the most fundamental right of individuals in relation to the state. You see, citizenship is irrelevant in this issue because once our government begins imprisoning individuals and trying them on secret evidence in a secret court, and in the absence of the defendant, then our government has established a precedent for itself. This precedent will then undoubtedly be embellished upon until our government brings this ominous power to bear on its own citizens—on *you*.

This is not a conspiracy theory, the facts are out there—and you need look no further than the laws being passed in your name. Our government has been doing this since at least 2002. It was in May of that year that then-Attorney General John Ashcroft announced, from Moscow, the arrest of one Jose Padilla, a.k.a. the "dirty bomber." The arrest took place one month prior to the announcement. Mr. Padilla was held incognito with virtually no contact with the outside world. He was never charged with a "dirty bomb" plot. And he was held without charge or trial for five years until a trial was granted him on completely unrelated charges to those for which he was originally accused. Mr. Padilla is a U.S. citizen, and was taken on U.S. soil.

*   *   *   *

Since our president has no qualms about destroying the principles of individual liberty on which our democracy was founded, it should come as no surprise that our government spied on us without warrants before Congress actually capitulated and sold us out, by making the warrantless wiretapping retroactively legal and expressly allowing the government to continue to use this tactic. Now, do you really believe that since they have been appeased on this front, certain elements of our government would stop there? Since they know that Congress is shaken with fear over *words*, why not just start searching peoples' homes without warrants—and planting evidence as they see fit? Do you really put this past them? Our government has trampled all over our rights and anyone who thinks they are going to stop voluntarily is deluded.

What about due process? By now everyone knows that the government is snooping on our private lives without court-ordered warrants. Specifically, I'm talking about these warrantless wiretaps. A warrantless tap is no different than a warrantless search of your home. Let's talk about the threat of planted evidence again. If government agents don't have to go before a court to prove their suspicions based on probable cause, they can just enter your dwelling, plant evidence of a crime and then arrest you based on the "evidence" found during that warrantless "search" of your home. How do you defend against planted evidence? You still don't think this can happen here? Just wait. Without the public's intervention, the laws will keep moving in that direction and soon no one will be safe from Big Brother.

This is no longer the America you grew up learning about in Civics class. The idealism that we were taught is no longer even a veneer, it has been completely wiped away in a coup from within. Those in power have taken our silent deference for granted for so long that they now feel that they can ignore us outright. And why not? We've unquestioningly accepted all of their rhetoric about freedom, while our eyes told the exact opposite of their words. We have done nothing thus far to even *try* to stop them, so why should they expect that we will do anything now?

But it is our responsibility to stop them. We have to remember that it is not only the right of the people to shrug off tyranny, it is our *duty*. If we can prevent tyranny from taking root in the first place, so much the better. And right now we are at such a critical point in our history. But in this crisis there is opportunity.

The Padilla case is an important illustration of what awaits you if we do not rein in our government. After years in solitary confinement, awaiting a military trial—a civilian U.S. citizen awaiting trial in a military court—the Supreme Court ruled that military law could not apply to Mr. Padilla and he could not be tried in a military court. So the government finally filed charges and tried him in Federal criminal court. But, again, they *never* charged him with the crime for which he had originally been arrested and detained. Since our system is based upon the presumption of innocence until guilt is proven, he must be assumed to be innocent of the "dirty bomb" allegation. Therefore, he was detained for years without charge or access to a lawyer based on bad-faith government claims that were never tried before a court of law. They eventually attained a conviction that could have been arrived at years before if the government hadn't been attempting to create a precedent allowing them to take any American off the street at their whim.

The government may not have been granted the formal precedent they desire by court ruling, but our current president, his cronies, and his cowardly enablers in Congress, have no problem codifying laws directly in contradiction to the words of the Constitution. This expansion of government power in the name of national security is more than just the first step to the destruction of our country, it is proof of the destruction itself.

Remember, evidence illegally obtained cannot be used against a defendant. Ask yourself this question: If evidence is uncovered of a true terrorist plot and the government uses illegal methods to obtain that, what then? If they are American citizens taken on American soil and the evidence, obtained illegally, cannot be used, they have to be set free.

This is the crux of it: *Actual* terrorists would have to be set free and never brought to justice because the government wants unquestioned authority over Americans' daily lives. And they want it without the drama of subjecting their desires to the assent of the American people. Such assent would require amending the Constitution, and I will address that in some detail shortly.

We can't lose sight of the fact that our government has detained several hundred people without charge for years on suspicions of terrorist activity, and they have only dared to actually put evidence before a court of law in a few dozen of those cases. Thus, we have evidence to prove that our government is so afraid of the light of day penetrating their schemes that they are willing to hold *any* person without charge indefinitely to avoid any public oversight whatsoever. They have done it before, and they are continuing to do it—in the name of fighting terrorism.

In order to understand terrorism, we need to define it. One dictionary definition of terrorism is: "The use of violence and threats to intimidate or coerce, esp. for political purposes"[1]. That is exactly the perfect definition to describe what our government is doing to our Republic. Aside from their proven power to take you off the streets at their whim, they have also been shown to fabricate outside threats for general consumption, with the intent to keep the public off-balance and afraid. The fear itself is exactly what they want—and they want it for only one reason: Their political ends.

I hope you have noticed that there is one thing our government *doesn't* keep classified: They want you to be afraid. Very afraid. They need you to fear the terrorists so you won't notice when they write and enact laws that strip you of your fundamental liberties and right to due process. It is important that you recognize that the final result of letting fear rule us is: *The terrorists win.* Yes, exactly what the government says they are fighting is exactly what they are visiting upon us. The terrorists are winning because our government officials would rather hide like cowards behind new unnecessary processes than uphold our rule of law. Terrorists use fear. And our government does, too. The exploitation of our natural fear of sudden death plays right into the hands of terrorists who hate our freedoms of religion, speech and our due process right to challenge our government.

$$*\qquad*\qquad*\qquad*$$

It's time we talk in detail about due process. What does that mean exactly? The 4th, 5th, and 6th Amendments deal with this specifically. While legal scholars might find others or disagree with my layman's interpretation, I am most concerned with the Bill of Rights and the fact that none of them have been overridden by subsequent amendments. So they are still the law of our land.

Here are the actual words written in the U.S. Constitution[2] concerning the rights that our government is usurping via the Military Commissions Act of 2006 and the Protect America Act of 2007:

Amendment 4:
The right of the people to be secure in their persons, houses, papers, and effects, against unreasonable searches and seizures, shall not be violated, and no Warrants shall issue, but upon probable cause, supported by Oath or affirmation, and particularly describing the place to be searched, and the persons or things to be seized.

Amendment 5:
No person shall be held to answer for a capital, or otherwise infamous crime, unless on a presentment or indictment of a Grand Jury, except in cases arising in the land or naval forces, or in the Militia, when in actual service in time of War or public danger; nor shall any person be subject for the same offense to be twice put in jeopardy of life or limb; nor shall be compelled in any criminal case to be a witness against himself, nor be deprived of life, liberty, or property, without due process of law; nor shall private property be taken for public use, without just compensation.

Amendment 6:
In all criminal prosecutions, the accused shall enjoy the right to a speedy and public trial, by an impartial jury of the State and district wherein the crime shall have been committed, which district shall have been previously ascertained by law, and to be informed of the nature and cause of the accusation; to be confronted with the witnesses against him; to have compulsory process for obtaining witnesses in his favor, and to have the Assistance of Counsel for his defence.

Why is it that so many people who have sworn to uphold these principles are now running from them as if they were some sort of suicide pact? I believe it is time that we force our leaders to take a real stand on the issue of constitutional rights. We must force them to state plainly their feelings about our individual liberties. It is obvious to me that they fear to do so publicly, so they pass unconstitutional statutes in the dead of night—without even reading them—so that they will be protected from being called "weak on terror".

There is a mechanism in the Constitution that allows them to rewrite these three important clauses: It's called amendment. The process of amendment can be time consuming, but it is there. If our politicians truly believe that we cannot afford the luxury of due process, let them state so publicly and for the record by doing it the right way—vote to amend the Constitution. Judging from the direction that the cowards in Congress and the criminals in the White House are going, the following would be a good choice of words for them to adopt:

The defense of the Constitution shall be conducted solely by the President and his appointed subordinates. The President shall have full authority to take whatever actions he feels necessary to preserve and protect this Constitution, including attacking foreign powers without the advice or consent of the Congress. Any statute or provision of this Constitution that shall in any way hinder his actions shall be disregarded at his sole discretion, without oversight from Congress or the

Courts. The President may restrict any person's access to the courts if he feels that such access would endanger this Constitution. The President, or his appointed subordinates, may introduce secret evidence at trial that the defendant and jury may be restricted from seeing; the defendant shall have no right to attempt to refute secret evidence presented by the government.

The President shall have the absolute right to Executive Privilege and Congress shall have no power to compel testimony from any person the President deems has information vital to this privilege. Congress shall have no right or power of oversight regarding the operations of the Federal government.

The President shall have full power to raise an Army, quarter soldiers, and detain without charge any United States citizen or other person apprehended anywhere in the world for as long as he feels necessary to preserve and protect this Constitution. The President shall have the authority to authorize any harsh physical treatment he deems necessary on any person in the custody of the government in order to obtain information necessary for the preservation of this Constitution.

A President, when signing any bill passed by Congress, shall have the authority to attach a statement to the bill when signing it into law. There shall be no limit on the President's use of this authority and the President's statement shall be binding on the law and the people, even if it directly contradicts the wording of the bill. Courts shall grant deference to the statement and hold it to have higher precedent than the bill passed by Congress.

Let's see Congress pass *those Amendments* by 2/3 vote of both houses and put it before the states for debate. I'm sure they will get few takers, although I really can't imagine why not, since they have already granted these powers and abdicated their authority through inaction and cowardice. Would anyone trust George W. Bush with this authority? Would you trust *anyone* with this authority?

If our representatives don't have the spine to introduce such laws in broad daylight by proposing these amendments, why should we feel comfortable that they have our best interests at heart when they furtively sneak them under the door like so many cockroaches at night?

But you won't see any of them with enough strength of conviction to stand up and do what their principles demand: Amend the Constitution to reflect the laws they are passing. They couch the abandonment of principle in lawyerly language and 40,000 pages of text in order to prevent the final, practical outcome from being easily observed: Abandonment of liberty. The Far Right is so full of righteous men, yet so few of them truly have the faith in their own political rhetoric to take action to its logical conclusion—*amend the Constitution*. I am personally glad for their cowardice in this regard, otherwise we would have already seen it done and we would be living in a police state (but that's not really too far off in the distance—if we fail to act now, it will become the way of life here in America).

*   *   *   *

Since our government, which is charged with protecting our lives, liberty, and property, is free to use fear to compel our submission to their betrayal of our nation, I hope you will allow me to demonstrate what this actually means to you. I beg your forgiveness in advance because the apparatus I choose to use for this is fear. I hope you understand that I do not take joy in using this tool, but as President Franklin D. Roosevelt said, "The only thing we have to fear is fear itself." Therefore, I employ it here to reveal that if we continue our capitulation to fear, we will be rendered helpless in the face of our own government. But if we recognize their tactics for what they are, we can overcome them, render them useless, and regain authority over our government.

In order to do this, I will need your willing cooperation. Lady Liberty is the birthmother of our nation, so I will use her as the person in my example. I do this because it is part of human nature to find it easier to endure hardship ourselves, than to witness someone we love endure the same hardship. I need you to keep Lady Liberty in mind at all times as we go through this exercise. This is an important factor in our fear: "I don't care what you do to me, just leave my family alone". Well, our government wants the power over all of us, and they will use whatever tools are available to gain that power—even if it means using our loved ones against us.

Because you are an American, you naturally interact with Lady Liberty all the time. So let's see what the government has in store for her. First of all, she will have to come to the attention of the government. How can that be possible, since she hasn't done anything wrong? Here's how. Americans' phone records are no longer private and the government has seized them, with the unquestioning submission of the telecommunications industry. Those records of who you contact, when, and from where are now in the government's hands, subject to data mining techniques. So what? Lady Liberty hasn't done anything wrong and has nothing to hide, so what does she have to fear from this? It is important to note that Lady Liberty is a vocal activist, often speaking at protest marches and loudly questioning the establishment, she also frequents the library where she borrows subversive literature like "Fahrenheit 451" and "Fahrenheit 9/11".

Because these phone and library records are collected by government agents without warrants, there was no showing of probable cause in their compilation. This means the government has no limits on how it uses the information gathered. And they are inventing "communities of interest" for them to keep a close eye on Lady Liberty—and justify the existence of huge and expensive bureaucracies. This is how a community of interest works: Anyone Lady Liberty has called or who has called her is in her "community".

This is not some form of benign social networking from MySpace or FaceBook, a community of interest, for government purposes, is everybody with whom a person talks or interacts. Lady Liberty's friends, acquaintances, business partners, and family members' calls are now tapped because the government wants to know why they would be talking to her.

So how does all of this actually bring your Lady Liberty to the attention of the government? The United States Department of State has an extensive list of charities that it considers to be "material supporters" of terrorism or terrorist organizations[3]. The State Department's argument for placing these organizations on a list of terrorist sponsors is that funding these associations allows other terrorist funding groups to divert money to carrying out terrorist attacks. It's a giant web, and any one of us can become ensnared in it.

Lady Liberty, being who she is has many friends. One of her friends, let's call him Mohammed, is a Muslim of Pakistani descent. He was born and raised in Great Britain (he has a British passport and an American wife). Because his parents, brothers, and sisters live in either Britain or Pakistan, he makes overseas calls and visits regularly. He also gives generously to charities that provide humanitarian relief to victims of natural disasters in Asia, such as the Indonesian tsunami of 2004 or the great Pakistani earthquake of 2005. These charities naturally provide services to Muslim populations (this is an important observation since any organization that does so is automatically suspected by the U.S. government). At some point, one of these Asian charities provided services to a community that has sympathy for radical fundamentalist Muslims. Since Mohammed has given money to an organization that has given humanitarian aid to people with such religious or philosophical leanings, Mohammed now is suspected of ties to terrorism.

Again, how does this impact our American Lady Liberty? Since her friend Mohammed is now on a terrorist watch list, his phone calls with Lady Liberty are now subject to wiretapping without a warrant by our government. Let's be clear about this: The phone call of an American is being eavesdropped upon by our government without even the fig leaf of a court order. You see, just because she has a friend who is a non-American, her phone calls with that person are now subject to government listening, for no other reason than the law now says that the other person doesn't have the same rights as she does. So her constitutional rights against unreasonable searches and seizures are curtailed to match those of the person of interest.

But it doesn't end there. Mohammed, because of his charitable contributions, is a person with financial "links" to a "terrorist organization". And the government wants to know why Lady Liberty is talking to that terrorist. Our government also wants to know of anybody else she might converse with on the phone. That places Lady Liberty—and you—and all of her (and your) contacts in her community of interest, suspected of terrorist ties.

It doesn't matter that Mohammed wasn't doing anything other than calling his family and giving to humanitarian charities. Your government has now labeled Mohammed and Lady Liberty—and you—as people with links to terrorism. You are now in the company of over 750,000 other American *citizens,* and others, who have been labeled as somehow "dangerous" by our government. Unnerving, I know. Out of 300 million people in America, our government considers three quarters of a million of them so dangerous that they have to be "watched." Congratulations, Lady Liberty has now joined their ranks, and taken you with her.

Lady Liberty likes to travel, so she goes to the airport to take a trip. Because she's on a watch list, she goes through extra security and an interview just to get on the plane. While she's being interrogated by her own government, for what she honestly doesn't know, all of her luggage is sifted through by an unscreened contract-TSA agent that's not making much more than $12 an hour.

Now she's had everything done to her except the cavity search (and we all know that is just a matter of time). She even suffers the indignity of x-ray technology that can see through her clothes, right down to the skin. After all of this, she finally gets on the plane. Safe in the knowledge that all of her inconvenience—and the violation of dignity—are well worth it to make sure she arrives at her destination safely.

While Lady Liberty is traveling, though, the government decides that it needs to know more about her. In a normal "pre-9/11 world" they would need a warrant to search her home. Not anymore. The 4th Amendment was one of the first casualties of the War on Terror. Now the FBI can conduct searches without disclosing the fact. Agents barely even need to tell their own boss. They do this through a mechanism known as a National Security Letter.

Because she's been labeled a person of interest, she's on that watch-list because she talks to bad people who give to charities the U.S. government does not approve of. So, even though she hasn't done anything other than befriend someone who happened to give to the wrong charity, the FBI is now snooping around in her house. If she has a landlord, they send him one of these National Security Letters, which requires him to allow them into her apartment in order to facilitate wiretapping. More on what the landlord can do about the National Security Letter in a bit. Keep in mind that it's a letter, from the executive branch, authorizing the executive branch to search your home for the purpose of placing equipment for electronic surveillance. It is *not* a warrant. But of course we all trust our government; surely they wouldn't do anything wrong or illegal while they are there.

But what if they did? Planted evidence is a reality, and it happens, particularly when the person doing the investigating is so sure of the "target's" guilt (that would be Lady Liberty—or you) that they can't be bothered with the formality of actually finding evidence to prove it. It's so much faster and convenient to just place it where it can be easily "found". This is where everything takes a very dark turn. Planted evidence in the form of computer files, papers, you name it, and suddenly Lady Liberty is much more than just a person of interest. She's *very* interesting now. This will prove to be an excellent technique for government agents to get rid of a vocal activist or "agitator", such as Lady Liberty tends to be at times. If she's lucky, she might get a trial, or have an opportunity to visit a judge at some point. But that's only if they decide to be gracious enough to even pretend to follow due process. The bad stuff comes when she's not appearing before a court.

Before we get into the details of Lady Liberty's ordeal, let's examine what happens when the other people that she knows and deals with start to draw the attention of our goon-squad government. What about all of her friends? You see, the community of interest doesn't just end with her (remember that you, dear reader, are now also in her community). Everyone she talks to is now of interest. The National Security Letters are insidious that way. They aren't warrants, so there is no requirement of a showing of probable cause to an objective body (a judge) that Lady Liberty has done something wrong. No, the National Security Letter is an assertion by the executive branch that a person is doing something that impacts our nation's security. So dangerous in fact that the other constitutional branches of government are considered to be a hindrance to the executive's efforts to safeguard the country, so they aren't consulted. These letters are an assertion that allows our government to go to Lady Liberty's employer and demand information about her. The letters are by their very nature secret, and it is a federal crime to talk about receiving one, so her employer can't tell her that the Feds are interested in her for some reason.

What happens after her employer has received this National Security Letter asking about her business dealings, travels, and communications? If she's like a great many Americans, she goes through annual performance evaluations of some sort for her job. These assessments are sometimes make-or-break opportunities for many of us, as they are the basis on which promotions, demotions, or even terminations are often founded. Now think about that for a second. If you're an employer, do you want employees around that the federal government is asking questions about? The obvious answer is, "No". Given this fact then, it is not out of the realm of possibility that Lady Liberty's employer might be less inclined to give her the positive review she needs to advance in her job, possibly forcing her out. This chain of events is based on the mere assertion, without an objective party to review the executive's determinations, that she is a "person of interest." The business world doesn't differentiate between person of interest and convict. It might as well be the same thing. All they know is that Lady Liberty spells trouble.

OK, so she lost her job or didn't get that well-deserved promotion. That's bad enough. But let's revisit the National Security Letter that was delivered to her landlord. Unless her landlord is some fan of the German Secret Police, it is most likely that he doesn't want this kind of trouble in his complex. That National Security Letter that her landlord can't talk about under penalty of federal law is trouble with a capital "T". How likely is it then that her lease will be renewed? Remember, she only has recourse if she's being discriminated against for being a member of a protected class—based on religion, sex, national origin, race—and being a person of interest is definitely not a protected class.

Let's take stock for a moment. Lady Liberty has either lost her job, or didn't get promoted, and now she's looking for a new apartment. She has essentially lost her job and her home, just because of who her friends are. Things couldn't possibly get any worse, right? You should know by now that we've only scratched the surface of what is going to happen to Lady Liberty, her family, her friends, mere acquaintances, and the grocery clerk that she just happens to know. Before we explore that, there is just one more scenario that needs to be investigated.

Lady Liberty has finally finished her trip, be it pleasure or business, and she's on her way home. She is stopped at the airport, let's say in Minneapolis, by officials from the Department of Homeland Security, or the FBI, or the TSA. It could even be agents from all of them. Anyway, she is stopped by a cadre of agents that have questions about her dealings that they would like her to answer. Being the law-abiding Lady Liberty that she is, she cooperates, up to a point, until she asks for a lawyer. At this point one of the other casualties of the war on terror becomes apparent: Her request for an attorney is denied.

Denied? But all American citizens are entitled to an attorney, right? I mean, it's in the Constitution (Amendment 6). Well not really, at least not anymore. You see, the Administration has dusted off an old phrase "enemy combatant". It's not really new. It was ripped from a Supreme Court decision from WWII[4]. It was a term used in what legal types call dicta or dictum, but that's not important. What is important for you to understand is that the term never showed up in the Court's ruling—the part that lays down the rule for that case, and future cases through precedent. No, the phrase was borrowed, and like so much else in our Global War on Terror, was reshaped to this Administration's fanatic ends.

The phrase "enemy combatant" is actually a "status" bestowed on Lady Liberty by the government—either the president or one of the minions he appointed during a Senate recess—that in essence strips an American citizen of all rights. This means that her citizenship status has been revoked; she has a new one now. Lady Liberty's status as a citizen has been suspended for the same reason that the government was tapping her phone, talking to her employer, landlord, and only the good Lord knows who else, because they think that she's a bad person. It's simply an assertion, because the Administration doesn't have to justify its classifications to anyone but itself. An interesting point about this is even if the government jumps through the circus hoops of a show hearing to determine her status as an enemy combatant, the body that would make that ruling (a Combatant Status Review Tribunal) doesn't have the authority to do anything other than rubber-stamp the government's claim that she's an enemy combatant[5].

Now back to the airport and Lady Liberty's predicament. She's been detained, and her status has changed. What is she to do? She will have plenty of time to think about it. I hope she likes extremely cold temperatures, small and enclosed spaces, and the sensation of drowning, because that is the world her new status has opened up for her: One where all of the rules we thought we knew, and tried to live by, are gone. She is now in a world where her status as an enemy combatant entitles her to all kinds of nice things, like those listed above, in addition to something called "extraordinary rendition". Sounds like an extreme sport or something, doesn't it? No, it's when our government intercepts one of us—U.S. citizen or not—and ships them off to a country other than the USA so that very bad things can be done to them. The only reason the government ships people elsewhere is because the pesky Constitution might still get in the way and grant them some inconvenient rights if they're in U.S. territory (but that's a *big* assumption). So they extraordinarily render Lady Liberty to somewhere like Romania, to a "black-site" outside of *anyone's* jurisdiction. No one knows where she is. Lady Liberty is alone.

While imprisoned at the black site, she experiences the worst of everything that man's inhumanity to man has to offer: Electric shocks, threatened mauling by dogs, and just plain old fashioned beatings, is what's in store for her. Just because she knew and talked to the wrong people, had the wrong name, or she was just in the wrong place at the wrong time. Or maybe it's because she chose to exercise her rights to challenge her government by participating in a war protest march, or checked out a book at the library. It could be any of these things, but it's most likely explanation is that we've all lost our minds to fear and we've allowed our government to run amok.

All of this just sounds so freaking crazy that right now you're probably scratching your head and wondering something along the lines of "When did this guy go off his meds and join the tinfoil hat club?" The sad thing is that I'm not making this up. All of these things *can* happen to our Lady Liberty—and *you*—because they *have* happened to other real people, Americans citizens or not. Our government has stopped American citizens at U.S. airports and held them, on continuously shifting—and legally questionable—grounds for years without access to a lawyer or family. Our government has mocked the judiciary and made a game of judicial procedure to its advantage at every turn, all the while strong-arming an increasingly cowed and complacent Congress into granting it immunity for violating our rule of law as defined by the Constitution. This has happened right under our noses, while we Americans have sat by and done nothing, except change the channel.

We did nothing when Canadian and German citizens, who just happened to have the wrong name and happened to be born in the wrong country, were picked up and "extraordinarily rendered" to locations like Egypt or Romania for torture. We torture people. I mean seriously, America *tortures* people. Stop and say that word out loud. Torture.

In the world I used to live in, that word would have made our stomachs turn as Americans, and even more importantly as human beings. Yet we are torturing people for information to keep ourselves safe. We torture for information that doesn't really exist. Information gained from torture is never reliable. And we are torturing people who don't have any real information to give because they are not terrorists—they are just people.

That is the fate that awaits your Lady Liberty—and you. One day, you'll be on a plane or in an airport. You're going to meet a pack of stern untrained, unscreened, and underpaid agents (they are most likely all of these things because they couldn't pass the psychological screening to even make it on a local police force, let alone the FBI). They have some questions for you. As you disappear from sight into an airport interrogation room, that's the last anyone will hear from you—and then you will disappear for real. You see, once we've crossed the line that says it's OK to torture, extraordinarily render, declare as an enemy combatant, *anybody*, we've crossed the line that prevents it from being done to you. You're on your own.

Standing up for your rights means standing up to those in power. And that means playing with a blazing fire. But to stand idly by and do nothing means watching a slow flame burn down your house. If you don't stand up for your rights, you can't defend the rights of Lady Liberty. She is alone.

✳   ✳   ✳   ✳

With this machinery in place, it is no longer enough to be an unquestioning "loyal American". This is so because loyalty implies that the ones we are following are worthy of our loyalty and that we have consented to their leadership. It is obvious from the 2006 midterm elections that the American people in general no longer consent to this leadership. But inertia is the key governing principle now. Our leaders can only govern because they are already in charge. We as citizens are not considered in their calculations. Now, because of continued safe redistricting and the existence of the Janus-faced political parties of the Democrats and Republicans, our leaders only pretend to listen to us every two years. And then they go about their happy business selling us down the river for the short term profits of their cronies—and their personal power.

Since we have discussed what these frightening new powers mean for us as individuals, let's examine what it means for us as a nation. From watching news programs on TV and reading the newspapers, we all know what our government is capable of, so the scenario I am about to unfold will not surprise you. Keep in mind that I don't necessarily believe that the following hypothesis is actually happening (or even could happen), I just want you to trust your senses and keep asking, "Would I put this past our government?"

First, we should follow the money. As I mentioned in an earlier chapter, the U.S. government is unable to account for billions and billions of dollars "spent" on the conflict in Iraq. There has been some speculation based on government waste of the past that the military doesn't actually spend $500 on toilet seats; they spend the normal wholesale price on the toilet seat and the rest goes to covert, off-the-books operations. I think that we would be safe to apply that same idea to our current profit-for-cronies-above-all-else government. Would you put the idea of funneling and hiding illegal payments to cronies through the pretext of war past the Bush Administration?

About those billions unaccounted for: Where could all that money possibly go? I don't know, do you? Will anyone in government give a straight answer to where the money went or even where the process broke down, allowing the loss of such huge sums of cash? It could simply be as it appears: Cash for cronies.

But I would like you to consider another piece of information. The Government Accountability Office estimates that 30% of all the small arms the United States shipped to Iraq from 2004 through early 2007, for the purpose of arming the Iraqi police and military, are unaccounted for[6]. That amounts to 190,000 weapons! Think about that number: 190,000 guns—and no one knows where they are.

In the U.S. military, each person is strictly liable to account for the whereabouts of his assigned weapon *at all times*. Any service member who misplaces a weapon, even temporarily, is subject to disciplinary action. If the weapon is outright lost, the service member can expect severe criminal penalties under military law, probably including time in Leavenworth. I have even seen people threatened with administrative punishment for misplacing a "rubber duck" (a fake, rubber rifle used in training).

The Department of Defense has developed some strict formal procedures for the dissemination of weapons to soldiers, sailors, airmen and Marines. When a weapon in the U.S. military changes hands, each person is required to confirm the serial number of the weapon and the receiving person is required to sign a document to confirm receipt and accept personal responsibility for that weapon. These formal procedures are in place because each weapon is a controlled item, and the military rightly takes the possession of and accounting for these weapons very seriously.

Given the fact that the military has admitted to losing *one hundred ninety thousand* weapons, does it sound like these procedures were strictly adhered to? Who is being held accountable for this? Obviously, someone along the paper trail lost control of these weapons. It shouldn't be hard to figure out who, where and when the breach took place. But rest assured: The military has started an "investigation" into it. That's code for, "We will take years to make the following determination: We don't know where they went and we can't find out, but we hope that you will lose interest and forget about this serious breach of our national security."

Before we combine these two facts, let's look at one more piece of relevant information: Private security contractors have been operating in Iraq without oversight or accountability since the invasion. So what, you ask? It's simple: Experience. These firms have gained priceless institutional knowledge—on our dime—in an active combat zone, including experience in operations and logistics.

So, what do we have here? These are the facts: a) A military exhausted from years fighting an endless and unnecessary war, b) Billions of dollars *in cash* gone, c) Hundreds of thousands of weapons missing, and d) Private security firms on the loose. I leave it to you to "connect the dots."

It isn't hard to reach a conclusion, is it? Now, I am not trying to propose a new conspiracy theory here. And I am certainly not trying to convince you that your government is creating a private army to use against you, because I'm not sure I personally believe that this kind of thing could happen. But such a thing actually happening is beside the point. The issue is: Would you put it past the cabal of zealots running the U.S. government to do it? Or to phrase it a different way: Do you trust the Bush Administration to *not* create a private army to use against you?

BETRAYED

The last chapter, as the title might indicate, was written in the hope that you will understand the fear our government is using in the Global War on Terror, and to recognize that our government has chosen to use that weapon against the American people. If you weren't made afraid by the contents of that chapter, I hope you were led to think a little bit about the endless possibilities of our government's excesses. At the very least, I hope you got a little bit angry.

This may seem romantic, but I believe that America is not just a physical border of longitudes and latitudes filled with commodities to be bought and sold. America lives inside us. Wherever we go, we are Americans. Anyone can be American. One does not have to be born within the physical confines of North America to be American. America is Liberty. Liberty is Eternal. America is Eternal.

America is and always was about Liberty. Our government was not founded for the few. It was founded for us all. Don't mistake that: I did not say that the few must defend it. All must defend it. From the Minutemen of our War for Independence to our Military Police in Afghanistan and Iraq today, Americans of all walks of life have stepped up to the challenge and honor of defending their homeland. Farmers from rural areas of the North and South stood together for what they believed in—and fought each other on fields of Blue and Grey. Right here, on our own soil, we fought *each other* for liberty. That kind of sword forged in fire cannot be defeated. Except when corroded from within.

Frighteningly, we seem to be approaching such a moment. This is the flash-point of our era: Either we stand together against tyranny or we spiral down into an American Dark Ages. The European Dark Ages lasted almost 400 years, but there is still time to prevent it happening here and now. Where there is life, there is hope. Our hope lies in the U.S. Constitution, and it yet breathes. It provides powerful tools for its own preservation; we must use them or lose them.

The U.S. Constitution contains language which requires members of the U.S. House of Representatives and U.S. Senate merely to take an oath to the effect that the member *"shall be bound by Oath or Affirmation to support this constitution."* From the first congressional session, beginning in 1789, members of both congressional Houses took this oath: *"I do solemnly swear (or affirm) that I will support the Constitution of the United States."* [1]

The current oath of office for members of the U.S. House of Representatives and the U.S. Senate reads as follows:

> *"I do solemnly swear (or affirm) that I will support and defend the Constitution of the United States against all enemies, foreign and domestic; that I will bear true faith and allegiance to the same; that I take this obligation freely, without any mental reservation or purpose of evasion; and that I will well and faithfully discharge the duties of the office on which I am about to enter: So help me God".* [2]

This oath bears close resemblance to the oath taken by all American military service members upon joining the military. Congressmen do not swear an oath to obey the president or officers appointed over them. Soldiers do. But just like congressmen, they swear to defend the Constitution against all enemies foreign and domestic, and they do so without mental reservation or purpose of evasion. Although I have resigned my Army commission, my commitment to that oath remains steadfast. While I will not necessarily obey the orders of the president or other officers, I will defend the Constitution against all enemies.

It is interesting to note that, according to the official United States Senate website, this oath was written for congressmen and senators during the 1860's— in the Civil War era—with the express intent to ensnare traitors[3]. It may have taken some time, but it looks like it finally worked. The majority of the people currently "serving" in our legislative branch have proven through their cowardice that they cannot be trusted with the preservation of our way of life. I feel confident and justified in arriving at such a harsh conclusion simply by observing their recent voting habits with regard to our fundamental principles.

American soldiers stand up to enemy firearms and roadside bombs every day—they fight *every day* for American liberty, while American politicians flee from mere words. They fear looking "weak on terror", so they vote to remove constitutional protections from the American homeland. They surrender to fear at home, while ordering others to fight for freedom overseas!

Two pieces of legislation prove that Congress has betrayed us, our forefathers, and our Constitution: The Military Commissions Act of 2006, which denies prisoners the right to contest their detention in federal court through the use of habeas corpus, and the Protect America Act of 2007, which gives the U.S. Attorney General the authority to spy on any—and every—American without a warrant and without any oversight by the courts. I challenge all readers to imagine you or someone you care about being caught in these unjust webs of governmental abuse—because if we let this stand, it will happen to you.

In approving these sweeping extra-constitutional powers for a president who already believes himself above our laws, Congress proved that they were more interested in going home on vacation than doing the work they had sworn to do—defend our Constitution. Some have argued that allowing representatives to go home to their districts is important so they can talk to their constituents—I will agree with that position. But in order to apply it to *this* Congress, one must make a big allowance—an assumption, if you will—about the motives of such elected representatives: One would have to believe that they are actually going home to understand the concerns of their constituents—that would be a very big ASS-umption.

Since long before the founding of our Republic, Americans have had a certain deep respect for the gravity which attends the taking of an oath of office. In some cultures, oaths are so serious that to dishonor an oath requires taking one's own life. There is a type of romanticism in it, certainly, but it nonetheless gives an honorable outlet for the shame of betraying that which one swore to uphold. One can imagine General Robert E. Lee, one of our country's greatest leaders, having the courage and sense of personal honor to do so. Can you name any of our current politicians that have the faith or the dedication for that brand of true honor? Do you know of any of them that would be the first to say "send me" or "send my daughter"? If so, vote for him.

My view is that something as vitally important as defending liberty justifies *not* taking an undeserved vacation. Please note that they did, however, see fit to pass the largest military budget in history (failing to account for the war in Iraq, of course), complete with pork-laden earmarks to ensure the satisfaction of their corporate masters. It seems that our soldiers are forced to fight in far off lands not to protect our collective liberty, but instead to protect the profits of a few well-connected contractors, while our politicians turn and flee from their sworn duties.

I believe it is important to highlight this point: Our politicians did not "cut and run" from the fight to prevent the usurpation of our liberties in the Protect America Act, they "turned and fled" from it. Cutting and running implies that they were actually engaged in a fight and then gave up. That is certainly not the case here: The mere *possibility* that someone *might* someday call them "weak on terror" struck such fear into their already quaking hearts that they turned tail and ran. They feared *words*. What brave leaders we have.

These cowardly politicians, who fear not only words but also action, need to be replaced. But that is not the main point that I am trying to make. I want to impress upon you—and anyone who will listen—that LIBERTY IS OUR GREATEST SECURITY. When you agree to surrender, however slightly, some liberty for the appearance of security, the government will encroach upon that up to the very limit and then demand more—because what power you give them will never be enough to "keep you safe". They will take and take and take until there is no liberty left to defend.

We must put a stop to it *now*. And it will take us working together as Americans to end it. I encourage you to keep in mind that the government can only assure you the appearance of security, because no one can ever guarantee you actual security. Life is full of danger and bad things happen—sometimes just by chance. We cannot allow this unacceptable power-grab by our elected servants to go unchallenged; it must not stand. *Where* are our leaders?

A dictionary definition of "leader" is "one that leads or guides"[4]. Where are our leaders? Instead of guiding us into our future, they look at what is around them and try to find the path most beneficial—and least resistant—to themselves and their financial contributors. They do so even if that means betraying long-term national strength for short-term individual popular approval. Sometimes, the hard choices have to be made and we should expect our politicians to make those hard choices unapologetically and based on principle, even if it means costing them their re-election. The hard choices sometimes mean immediate and unpopular sacrifices, but a true leader can inspire people to great feats of collective accomplishment based upon such sacrifices. Do you know of any elected "leaders" capable of such feats today?

Since liberty is worth dying for, I expect those who seek public office and swear to uphold the Constitution to do everything up to and including that just that: Dying for it. If soldiers swear to defend liberty with their lives, and receive substantially fewer benefits than elected officials do, I do not find it unreasonable to insist that government officials who make our laws have the same level of commitment. If a politician is not willing to sacrifice everything: His life, fortune and sacred honor for We the People, he should not be in a position of authority, nor should he have a title which even implies "leader". Where *are* our leaders?

A true leader is "first in, last out". A true leader ensures his followers have what they need, even if it means he must go without. A true leader works alongside his followers to retain within himself the actual soul of his people. Does this remind you of any particular politician currently seated or running for office? Off the top of my head, not a single name comes to mind. Where are our *leaders*?

When a politician surrenders principle to fear, he emboldens our enemies. It has been said many times that our enemies hate us for our freedoms. As cliché as that sounds, it's not too far off the mark. Our liberties define us and strengthen us. Diversity is the cornerstone of our success; America really is the melting pot of the world. Our enemies want us to live and think as they prescribe and when our government officials, in the name of physical security (which they cannot guarantee), vote to undermine any liberty, they give considerable aid and comfort to those enemies. And by doing so, they hand the terrorists a victory that could never have been achieved by force.

As easy as it is to blame cowering and quaking politicians, the hard part comes when we realize that they have the full authority to speak and act in our name. Through their fear, they make us all look weak and fearful. When people meet with our representatives, they are, in fact, meeting with us. Our politicians are those whom we have chosen to represent us. If you cannot point to your representative (or even name him) and say that you are proud of him and that he truly does speak for you, then you can only conclude that it is time for a change. If you are not proud of those that represent you, you must work to elect someone you can be proud of.

Remember, as a nation, We the People are responsible and must answer for the mistakes of our elected politicians. How would we explain our shame to the many tens of thousands of men and women who have given their lives for the ideals of our country, now that Congress has taken the steps to destroy those very ideals for which they sacrificed? Keep that in mind the next time you hear a politician speak about sacrifice and the greater good. But we haven't heard that kind of language from a politician in this country for a very long time.

*   *   *   *

If I were to die today, I would not die as free as the day I was born—and I was born while Nixon was in office. That's saying something. I have worn my country's uniform and I have gone to war for my people, yet today my countrymen and women are less free than they were the day I took my first breath. Why?

Americans are not a fearful people. Americans do not, have not, and will not live in fear—*never*. It is simply not in our nature. We fight for truth; we like to see the underdog fight against insurmountable odds and win because we know it can be done—we as a people have done it time and again. Americans win because our ideals are solid. We do not compromise on liberty.

So why do those we elect to high office insist that we must do so? Why do we allow ourselves to be forced to surrender to fear? I refuse to live my life in fear of cowardly terrorists, and I equally refuse to surrender one ounce of liberty to American politicians who have forgotten what America is really about: Liberty. We can only lose by abandoning those ideals. Historically, we have not tolerated politicians who surrender to anything, let alone fear—until now.

Liberty does not mean living without risk. Liberty *requires* risk. Liberty, to me, is the right to live my life as I see fit, without someone monitoring my phone calls, my correspondence, and my bedroom. To live in peace with those around me—to exercise my liberty without harming someone else's right to do the same thing. Certainly, there are prices to pay for liberty—you must be willing to fight for it. Liberty is so easily taken away, that we must be ever vigilant. I think of it as "responsible liberty". I have no problem with making sacrifices for my own liberty and that of my family, friends and neighbors. It boils down to this: I protect your liberty, you protect mine.

But I will not sacrifice liberty itself in the name of being protected against terrorists. Lack of liberty is too terrifying a thought by itself; death would be preferable. Benjamin Franklin, one of our earliest, wisest and greatest patriots is famously quoted: "Those who would give up essential liberty to purchase a little temporary safety deserve neither liberty nor safety."[5] He was right. And our politicians are banking on us forgetting the duty that we owe to ourselves that those words create.

If defending liberty can mean one's death, then every act to preserve liberty which results in less than death must also be pursued. There is nothing the government or anyone can give you that would be worth the sacrifice of liberty itself—you fight and die if necessary to preserve it, anything less is mere surrender.

*   *   *   *

Americans do not suffer loss well. We like to win. And we play by the rules. So why are we allowing our politicians to surrender on our behalf? Our sometimes aggressive methods to win have led some to refer to us as the "ugly American". And there is no denying that there are some of us who fit that stereotype. However, as a people, Americans are by and large anything but "ugly". We are more than a nation, we are a family: We take care of each other—and we defend each other. We care. We care about each other and we care about our rule of law. That is the true beauty of America. It is the liberties that we guarantee for one another that have allowed us to thrive thus far.

I can just hear some conservative blow-hard writer clickity-click on his keyboard condemning this "soft liberal" for "caring", but I am unconcerned with the semantic prejudices of the hypocritical Right. I also know that despite their personal desire for moral authority over me, I am nonetheless one who put on the uniform to fight for their right to invent "facts" as they like. But they need to keep in mind that I also fought for my own right to speak the truth as I see it— and I have only begun to do so.

I have chosen to speak now because lives are on the line! We do not have time for partisanship. Republican, Democrat, liberal, or conservative, these labels are meaningless. The only label that matters is: American. Everyone must be a part of the process of retaking our country or we will lose. As citizens, our first action must be to demand an answer from our government: Who is really in charge here?! (For those politicians that will try to answer, be warned: What you say will be taken for the record and it *does* matter).

Are there no leaders left in our government? A leader does not turn and flee. As I said before, turning and fleeing must be distinguished from "cutting and running", since the latter implies engagement. No. This democratically elected Congress of whores turned and fled when they saw the threat of being branded "weak on terror". They were too afraid to even *pretend* to stand their ground. Cowardice in a leader is nothing less than treason. If our soldiers are sworn to die for their country, the oath that an elected official takes should be just as binding. A soldier who runs from a fight is humiliated; a politician who runs is rewarded with re-election. What a disgrace: There are higher principles than mere election.

We insist that our police, firemen, military personnel, teachers, and even bus drivers, have integrity. Why do we not expect and demand the same from our elected servants? These are the people who make the laws which mandate accountability in all of these other positions. Why can't we find people who can live up to the laws they impose on the rest of us? They impose ethics laws that professionals and others have to obey, but their own ethics are DOA when they get on the Hill. What sort of integrity is it that makes someone keep looking out for only himself or the narrow interests of his party?

In our current political environment, we have a Left so fearful of being "soft" that they have actually become weak. And now their moderate stands amount to retaining the status quo—what kind of liberal is that?! The status quo is one of ever-shrinking economic opportunities for the average American, and of quickly eroding rights of public dissent and personal privacy, not to mention unnecessary expeditionary military adventures to steal natural resources from others around the world.

If we want to break away from the world which our leaders have created, then we have no choice but to hold our "representatives" accountable. It is time we regain control of our government. Right now we are in the clutches of two dying political parties, fighting each other for the spoils from the wreckage they have created of our grand American experiment. The only answer is to look to ourselves. Since these two parties have created the crisis we now face, we cannot look to them to correct it.

But if we are going to try to save our country, we need to ask: Is the Constitution worth saving? That's the real question that faces us today. It is under attack from the Far Right and undefended by the Left. The middle is disenfranchised and exploited because neither side cares what they want.

The only answer I can find is, "Yes, the Constitution is worth saving". But what sacrifices will we willingly make to preserve it? What sacrifices will the government force upon on us if we don't preserve it? Keep in mind that liberty is our only security. Without it, the government will take by force of law from you whatever their cronies want. Without the guarantees of liberty and privacy guaranteed in the Bill of Rights, we have nothing to defend.

In order to defend our liberties, though, we must first recognize that those liberties are based on our rule of law—and vice versa. It is a fundamental principle of our law that evidence obtained illegally cannot be used in a criminal case. Intelligence can be used to stop a terrorist, but intelligence is quite different from evidence. Intelligence is designed to inform—and protect—evidence is amassed to prove culpability. If these two concepts become interchangeable in our system, no one will be safe; whatever those in power want, they will get. Does this sound like self-government to you?

*　　　*　　　*　　　*

At the beginning of this chapter, I reprinted the oath that members of Congress take when entering office. To all of them I say: "You have betrayed your oath to us as a people and by so doing you may have damned us all. I can only hope that the first half of that statement is uttered as sentence is pronounced for your crime of treason. The American people are the ones who have suffered for your madness, and we are rightfully angry at the injustice we have endured at the hands of those we elected to uphold and protect our Constitution from all enemies, foreign and domestic".

Our Constitution creates a system that is designed to keep us safe as a community. That Constitution is at its core a social contract that keeps us together as a nation. In order for this contract to function, it is essential that those we have selected as its defenders fulfill the commitments and obligations that are necessary to protect it. The contract calls upon us as a nation to secure the common welfare for everyone. Yet at every opportunity our leaders have turned their backs on that fundamental purpose of our community. And for what? That is the subject of the discussion to follow.

Frank Herbert wrote that power does not corrupt, power attracts the corruptible. That is exactly what has taken place in Washington, DC. As a center of immense power, our nation's capital is rife with corruption and our people's House has been turned into little more than a convenient den for modern-day money changers. It is not only politicians that slither inside the halls of our Congress. Like so many cockroaches, big-Pharma, big-Defense, big-Ag also skitter through those chambers, with great and ill effects for our Republic. These parasites peddle the one thing that our politicians need the most—money. Money that will help them fight the only war that really matters to them: The War for Power.

Once politicians have the power that their corrupt souls so desperately crave, their only thought is to maintain their grip. In order to do so they have devised a system that grants us a choice between their two chosen parties. Every single election season, we have the exact same thing in a red or blue package. Each election cycle we are expected to become excited to great passion about candidate D or R. And we have obediently obeyed their wishes over the past century.

There is a reason that George Washington, you might remember him, one of the founding fathers of our country, warned us as a nation over 200 years ago against political parties. Why? The answer is simple: Political parties divide the nation. These parties serve as a distraction and a proxy in a giant gladiatorial struggle for the control of the levers of power—nothing more. Every modern democracy uses a party system. Political parties can be a positive way for like-minded people to band together to raise their voices and effect change. But our two-party system has grown so corrupt that there is no way to actually tell the two apart—they are the two sides of a corporate coin. And the Democratic and Republican parties in the United States do not seek to unite us in common cause, they seek to divide us for their own ends.

Both parties push us to cheer for one or the other gladiator in the political coliseum every two to four years. They choose the two people we can vote for. It's as simple as that: Two private political parties (and yes, they are private organizations) tell us our choices. If we ever threaten to vote for someone else, we will hear, as Kodos said in a Simpson's episode, "Go ahead! Throw your vote away!"

We have been throwing our votes away on incompetent and corrupt politicians for decades now (do I need to remind you that Richard M. Nixon and George W. Bush have both held our nation's highest office?) But imagine if we all decided to go ahead and "throw our votes away" on some third-party or independent candidate in the next election. You would see a seismic shift in our political landscape—and overnight. That's the power that We the People truly have over events in our country. We should consider *using* that power sometime in the very near future.

You will often hear from someone running for office that they seek to end "politics as usual". However, once they get into office and see how the system has been set up to protect their incumbency, they instantly lose the desire for the change they championed on the campaign trail. The parties continue to govern only with their next re-election in mind. Decisions are not made based on a reasoned policy process with an eye to the best outcome for all involved. Instead we have a continuous jockeying within the legislative process to curry favor with one private special interest group over another, and "Drum roll please … The winner is: The highest bidder!"

Whereas consensus is clearly possible on a large majority of issues facing this country like the national debt or social security reform, to name just two, the parties' political theater is designed specifically to prevent people from coming together and developing workable solutions to these problems. The system is set up arbitrarily by the two parties in power to force us to use their binary Republican/Democratic way. By so doing, their parties divide us as a nation, and thus they have violated the fundamental precept of the Constitution—community. And so, we are left, as New York Times columnist, Frank Rich, said so eloquently, "know[ing] that the ideals that once set our nation apart from the world have been vandalized, and no matter which party [we] belong to, [we] do not see a restoration anytime soon."[6]

The examples of how our "leaders" have divided us are many. One party in particular, however, has used the prospect of gays in the military, classroom, and bedroom as a means to frighten voters to the polls for years. And that is really what the Don't Ask Don't Tell policy is—just a red herring designed to distract and to divide Americans one from another through fear, where otherwise there would be no division. We all know who I'm talking about here, yeah, it's the Republicans. Fear about gay marriage and gays in the fox hole were one of the primary motives that pushed the so-called "values voter" to the polls in the 2004 election. Is anybody going to be really surprised when they try to do it again and again in the years to come? As despicable as their tactics are, they have proven to work. Why should we expect them to abandon something that gets them what they want?

While the Don't Ask Don't Tell policy is just one example of how our leaders have betrayed us, there are many, many others that warrant mention. Things have gotten so out of hand that this American doesn't know where to turn anymore. I come home after a year of ostensibly protecting the "American way of life" only to find that which I was supposed to be protecting has been destroyed by my government. I realize that sounds a little harsh, but I believe that a brief recitation of the crimes of this Administration with the assistance of a cowering Congress will bring you to the same conclusion.

My fellow Americans, let us start off with the biggest crime of them all—the lie that is the Iraq War. As of the day that I'm writing this, late in the fall of 2007, the United States military has found no weapons of mass destruction created by the Hussein regime. We were told that Iraq was a threat to us because the regime had chemical and/or biological agents, and that they were capable of delivering those weapons and causing massive casualties here, in the United States. We have since learned that all of the assertions of imminent danger posed by Hussein and his WMD, was just so much hot air. Hot air that the Bush Administration, coupled with the assistance of his congressional enablers, eagerly used to inflate our fears after the 9/11 attacks to justify this war. Let me say it once again—*there were no weapons of mass destruction in Iraq*. Sanctions worked. So, if you're not pissed off about the lie that got us into this disastrous war in the first place, I'm assuming that someone bought you this book as a gift, and good for them. That lie, in and of itself, should be enough to make everyone angry.

If only we could end the list of reasons for being angry with that one lie. Unfortunately, that is not the case. The lies about this war don't end with the one that got us into it. We were lied to about the cost and consequences of the war as well. Who can forget the now infamous words of Lord Darth Cheney himself when he said "We will be greeted as liberators"? What about Donald Rumsfeld and that classic line of his about the war taking "weeks rather than months"? (Remember, I was sent to Iraq from the Inactive Reserve three years after the war began because "We have to fight with the Army we have, not the Army we want or wish to have"). And who could forget about Paul Wolfowitz with his, shall we say "rosy," estimates as to the cost of the war and the capacity of a quickly reconstituted Iraqi government, flush with newly flowing oil cash, to repay the cost? Each and every one of these statements not only turned out to be mistaken, they were patently false by design. But the reality-based community was ignored in the headlong rush to war by politicians who were too cowardly to actually go into combat themselves when the opportunity presented itself in Vietnam.

Not only were they lying when they said we would be greeted as liberators, and when they said we'd be done in six months, our leaders are still lying to us about it today. They refuse to put the cost of the war in the ordinary Pentagon budget, opting instead to use emergency funding bills, as if there was no way to foresee that they would need more money for the war. These smoke and mirror tactics are becoming wearisome. But that may well be the point: If they just keep doing the same thing over and over again, maybe the American people will just stop caring. Would you trust them to do anything differently?

By lying I mean they are absolutely refusing to acknowledge the need for some sort of sanity in the fight against terrorism, so that we can plan for the future of our military and nation. Every opportunity has been presented to the Administration to lay out some sort of timeline, roadmap, series of milestones, any form of bread crumbs even, for bringing this nightmare to an end. And every single chance for such a thing has been dismissed as defeatism. Yet so many people fail to recognize that hope is not a strategy.

All of this anger is directed at those who recognize the dangers that are headed our way, but for fear of "looking weak on terror" refuse to do anything about it. I know I'm just a former 1st Lieutenant who served a year in Iraq, what could I possibly know compared to the political hacks running the Pentagon? I've seen the cracks in our national security strategy myself. Hell, I ended up falling through one those cracks by being called back years after my term of service was complete; that recall just proved that the Pentagon was trying to stave off disaster by one more rotation. Luckily, I'm not the only one pointing out the biggest reason we really need to get out of Iraq: It is looming ahead for our military—complete breakdown.

We've been hearing it for months that our armed forces are almost out of the resources they need to function at a minimum, let alone fight a six month war morphed into almost six years now. As I was writing this book in late November 2007, I received word from a buddy that got home from Iraq at the same time I did, in April of 2007. He has already been recalled again for another tour in the Sandbox. He has been home for only seven months and has already learned that he will be sent back to Baghdad.

Rotations back into combat after very short periods at home with family is just one reason that our military is becoming exhausted with the pace of operations in Iraq and Afghanistan. Our armed forces are becoming overextended because soldiers are not re-enlisting and officers are leaving as soon as their period of service is complete. The recruits we find to replace those we are losing are barely enough to keep us at current strength, let alone sufficient to increase the size of our military.

This is the dirty truth that they don't want to talk about, but it's there. And this lie is just a continuation of the one they told us when they said that our troops had all the gear that they needed. If that is true, why were soldiers having to "up-armor" their vehicles by themselves with material from junk yards? If our military really was in such great shape, and they were taking care of our citizen-soldiers like they should, why were military families forced to spend personal resources to send their soldiers body armor for protection? Why? Because the Administration and this Congress talk a big game about supporting our troops, but in the final analysis they're still just lying to us.

When I was in Iraq, the first combat brigade to which I was attached, the 172nd Stryker Brigade Combat Team, had their tours extended for three months so that they could go to Baghdad to take part in Operation Together Forward. Some were in the air on their way home, when the order was announced. They literally turned the plane around in flight to get them back to Iraq. Sounds like really supporting the troops, eh? But it gets worse.

The concept of Operation Together Forward was that U.S. Army units would partner with Iraqi Army units to work on securing Baghdad (this was the summer before the Surge was even thought of). Well it turned out that Baghdad had such a reputation for intense violence that some of the Iraqi Army units refused to deploy there. Here is what I wrote in a letter home on September 6, 2006 regarding this very event:

> *I try to avoid making any normative statements (or pontificating) about the war in these letters, but I think I need to mention a general feeling that we have here regarding what's going on. It has subsided, as most things will do here, but many people were/are very angry (myself included) at the news that certain Iraqi Army units have refused deployment to Baghdad. Our guys in the 172nd Stryker Brigade Combat Team were kept here longer than their planned tours to go to Baghdad to serve in "Operation Together Forward". How can it be "together" if the Iraqi's aren't interested in being involved?! Why is it that they are allowed to refuse to serve—in their OWN country—when our guys' plane is turned around in mid-air to come back?! Sec Rumsfeld said of our guys that "they volunteered, they want to do this." That may or may not be true, but the Iraqi's ALSO volunteered for their Army—they don't have a draft—so what plausible reason can be given for us to keep fighting for them when they won't fight for themselves?!*

✳   ✳   ✳   ✳

If we take the Global War on Terror as more than a mere bumper sticker slogan (I know, that's a stretch, but humor me), then we have to recognize that Iraq had nothing to do with terrorism directed at the United States. We know that terrorists will use whatever weapon is available to do us harm, and will use whatever means available to deliver that weapon. So, if we are going to fight this "global" war, the first step would naturally be to secure our borders by inspecting all of the cargo that enters our country in pursuit of the almighty dollar. But—and don't be surprised at this—that was determined to be too expensive. Protecting Americans in the United States is too expensive when weighed against fighting a war against a country that did not attack us. Can you see the pattern here? Those charged with keeping us safe have made the calculated decision that commerce is more important than safety here at home and profits are more important than ending wars overseas. This is the essence of the Global War on Terror. You are justified to be angry at this. You *should* be angry at this.

I touched on this in a previous chapter, but it demands repeating: The ongoing lie of the war gets even worse when you consider how we're paying for it. The short answer is, we're not, at least not right now, and certainly never in any way that a country has ever paid the costs of fighting a war before. All of the spending has come in the form of supplemental spending bills or emergency allocations.

Add to this the fact that our "leaders" have done perhaps the dumbest, and certainly most unprecedented thing ever during war: They've cut taxes! So let's get this straight, our leaders are borrowing money from someone, mostly the Chinese (our biggest rivals and competitors for oil by the way), who are happy to give us enough rope to see if we will hang ourselves with it, all so they can pay for the war while cutting taxes. Apparently, this president and Congress really do believe in Voodoo economics, because this makes no sense.

In essence then, the first of many reasons that warrant American outrage toward this Administration is the fact that we were lied to. Our leaders lied about the threat that Iraq posed to us, and they lied about the cost of the war—and they continue to do so. Our leaders lied about the state of our military then and now. Our leaders lied to us about when our troops would be coming home. Our leaders will keep lying to us as long as we allow them to do so. Yet the lies and causes for outrage just continue to grow. But where is this outrage? I read of it regularly in the newspaper, but I don't see it. I admit that I can feel it when I hear people speaking, but what are they doing about it?

The cost of war is not just in money. It can also be measured in lost opportunities. The money spent on war could (and probably should) be spent to protect our homeland directly through better screening of cargo, better educational opportunities for everyone, maintained infrastructure, or virtually any number of worthwhile peace-time activities (even paying down the national debt so that we don't saddle future generations with our greed). But, again, the cost is not just in money. We are losing our national honor and our national tradition of liberty.

While our leaders have been working overtime to keep their lies about the war up and running, they have also been steadily stripping away the protections at home. We need to take them to task for their crimes. I'm talking about the Patriot Act, Patriot Act II, the Military Commissions Act, the ... The list of Acts that destroy Americans' freedoms goes on and on. Just in October of '07, almost the entire House of Representatives, 404 of them to be exact, voted for a piece of legislation to understand and expose violent extremists here at home. Sounds like a noble cause, but that's what the doublespeak that comes out of Washington these days is supposed to make you think. The House approved H.R. 1955—an Act that would make it a crime to think about things like removing the president from office, let alone a revolution.

As of this writing, this Act is not yet law, as it has yet to be considered by the Senate. But that's not the point. 404 of your congressmen feel so threatened by you being able to speak your mind that they have decided to allow an unaccountable bureaucracy to enforce penalties against extremist thought crimes. Think about that: Just thinking and speaking about holding elected officials accountable for their crimes could be considered extreme.

You see, the written purpose of the legislation is to understand why someone would turn to terrorism in America. Again, sounds like a good idea, right? Yet the language they used, such as "extremism" and "violence", are so vague in the wording of the law, as to encompass nonviolent protest and civil disobedience. Through the passage of this bill, our Congress has put the final touches on the machinery to turn every American into an extremist, if not outright terrorist. The bill defines violent radicalization as "the process of adopting or promoting an extremist belief system for the purpose of facilitating ideologically based violence to advance political, religious, or social change"[7]. The bill only uses the word "violence" as cover for the "research" which will result in the eventual definition of extremist belief. But how they intend to define "extremist belief system" should already be obvious: It is whatever those in government want it to be, especially if you're advancing political, religious or social change to loosen their grip on power.

Given that fear is the weapon of choice of terrorists and that loud and public dissent is the traditional cornerstone of our system, this legislation seeks to effect political change by making you fear to dissent. Thus, one can only arrive at this logical conclusion: By passing this legislation, the United States House of Representatives has engaged in domestic terrorism. They have turned the War on Terror into a War *of* Terror—and their target is none other than the American people themselves.

At this point, I think it would be appropriate to relate a personal experience regarding the government's use of the word "extremist". I went to an anti-war rally in Salt Lake City in October 2007. One of my companions noticed an inordinate number of police there. He asked one of the policemen why there were so many for such a small protest, and the policeman replied, "Because extremists like you might open their mouths." You see? That is exactly what this legislation hopes to accomplish: Letting the government decide which thought or word is extreme and thus giving them reason to silence it.

This bill recognizes that terrorists can be anyone, even you or me. Therefore, so the reasoning goes, the government needs to know more about you, and the groups you participate in, because you could be a terrorist. In their zeal to label Americans as terrorists, to keep us all safe of course, where does the line get drawn?

We crossed that line before, for those of you old enough to remember, when Nixon was president. We had an enemy list operating out of the White House then, and we've got one now. The language "extremist" is deliberately vague so they can catch up whomever they want in their net against "extremism." Given this Administration's outright contempt and loathing for dissent—you might remember the vice president's "aid and comfort to the enemy" line about those who disagreed with the war—and it's not difficult to imagine that anyone who has had the audacity to publicly and vehemently disagree with government actions or policies will be labeled an extremist.

Again, think about it for a second. We've already got the FBI snooping around libraries and trying to get your reading records. The government is already tapping God-only-knows whose phone and now they are going to try to define extremist and learn what makes people turn to extremism? I'll tell you the answer right now, and they can give me the $20 million allocated for H.R. 1955.

The thing that turns people in America into extremists is an unresponsive government that is more concerned with lining the pockets of its members and their cronies than they are about the business of governing. This is not an extremist statement, it's fact—just look at the history of our Republic. The founders had to resort to the extreme act of declaring their colonies independent from just such a government. When holding our government to account and replacing them for their crimes is labeled an extremist idea, then I believe it becomes time to turn the tables and label the government itself extremist.

The fact that a lobbyist has an easier time meeting with our representatives than the average citizen does, has probably made many of us into "extremists". A government that won't do something as simple as mandate higher fuel efficiency standards in our cars because the manufacturers don't want to invest in the technology that would get us off foreign oil has made many of us into extremists. The fact that our parents are retiring and the Social Security system may or may not support them—while our Democratic and Republican Nero's fiddle—has turned some of us into extremists. I hope that you get the point. The fact that your government considers you an extremist for disagreeing with it should piss you off to no end. If it does, be sure to keep it to yourself though, you wouldn't want somebody at the FBI to think that you are an extremist.

I realize that this chapter paints an angry picture of America, and perhaps of myself. Some might say that to be so angry is unhealthy. I would be inclined to agree with those who would say so—to some extent. However, righteous fury and anger are what we are talking about here, and it's well past time for both of them. Additionally, anger is only a problem if you leave it at that—anger—and don't do anything with it. You see, if all you are is angry, you're most likely just covering up for some other emotion, like fear or frustration (both rather understandable emotions to experience given the current situation). That's the problem if you just stay pissed off. That's why I had to write this book. I could no longer remain just angry. I had to do something about it. Now the question is, will you?

COMFORT ZONE

A standard defensive tactic is to form a protective ring around the middle. In the middle rest those most in need of protection: People and resources. As a result of this protection, the middle is made safe, relative to the environment around it. This principle underlies the premise of a strong national defense mechanism. We project our force outward from the center in order to protect our people and resources in the homeland. Our nation's assumption of this defensive posture requires America's citizens to answer this question: Who or what are we protecting? We? Who is this "we" of whom I speak? As in: Who among us—here in the comfort zone of the middle—is going to do the protecting? We must answer this question because, first off, we need to know that which we seek to protect before we can do so, and secondly we must understand that protecting the middle requires us to turn outward from the center in order to face that which threatens us.

Turning outward will require that all of us get out of our personal comfort zones. This will mean more than just speaking out—although that will be vital—it will require you to question everything you hear. You will have to think critically at all times. You cannot trust what anyone in government says anymore. They have lost, for the time being, that benefit of the doubt. So many authority figures have made so many false claims lately that not one of them can be above suspicion now. Therefore, you will be required to hold them to defend with facts their public assertions. We can no longer afford to simply accept what they say at face value; they have proven their deceitfulness.

I know that many people feel that their local politicians are above the types of deception that we see on the national scene. I happen to believe this as well. But we can give no quarter to those that we entrust with our governance. They must be held constantly answerable to us. It is unfortunate that we have to confront our local, trusted officials, but that is the price we must pay—eternal vigilance requires that *every* government representative, elected officer or appointed bureaucrat be suspect. Those with actual power over our lives can be given no latitude to deviate from our principles.

When I first started writing this book in August of 2007, I wanted it to be a call for Americans to begin patriotic action and retake our country. But I realized that the first step to action is to move beyond our everyday routine and to break out of our individual comfort zones, and that's where I got the title for this chapter. As I was finishing up the book in November, Barack Obama, as a primary Democratic presidential candidate actually used the phrase "comfort zone" on NBC's Meet The Press. My first reaction was "Oh no! I have to change the title of my final chapter". But then I realized that his embrace of this concept is proof that its time has come. It has never been my desire to try to reinvent the wheel with this book—I just want to highlight what Americans must do. And taking *action* is definitely the most important thing we must do right now.

I don't know if Senator Obama will continue to use the phrase or even the concept of this in the coming months, but the fact that a presidential candidate recognizes, as I do, that it is time for Americans to actually become engaged in their self-governance, proves that I am not alone in this observation. But the big question is: How?

In that interview, the senator was focusing specifically on the Democratic Party engaging evangelical Christians. That's a good start, but it's not the whole pie. We Americans must engage each other *regardless* of our specific interest groups. And not just from the perspective of our individual comfort zones, but from the perspective of shared sacrifice. What is required of us to save our country? My call is for everyone to engage everyone else. We must specifically seek to connect with people who do not agree with us. Not just Democrats engaging evangelicals or Republicans reaching out to anti-war activists. We cannot have any preconceived notions about what the other guy has to say—we need to find out for ourselves by letting him say it. The only thing you should be concerned with is the fact that we are all in this collectively and if we don't stick together, we *will* be torn apart.

A natural result of turning from our comfort zone is a sense of unease, tension, or fear. However, we must look beyond this fear within ourselves—as we face those who threaten us—and look to those who will come after. Our duty is to them. We cannot leave this country worse off than we found it. We cannot idly lament the slow flickering death of liberty's flame at the heart of our nation. Our government would have us believe that the sacrifice of these liberties is essential, and all that is required of us, to defend our nation. We do not have the luxury of standing by as our liberties are destroyed in order to protect them. To simply allow our nation, bereft of its guiding light of liberty, to stumble in darkness toward the abyss, would be our greatest failure. It would be a failure of our moral compass, and a betrayal of our duty to future generations. We live in a time of urgency, and we cannot allow cowards whose only weapons are words of fear, to divide and defeat us when no manner of steel could do the same.

The most effective way to defend liberty's flame is with the roaring wind of our collective voice, raised in protest against the cowards who hide freedom's light behind a veil of secrecy, depriving liberty of essential fuel—the knowledge and consent of the governed, when we need it most. Our voice of protest must be the breath on the smoldering ember that reignites our nation's passion for its peoples' freedoms. That is why I make this point with my book—it's not about me, it's about the message. Whatever fate has in store for me, the message—and America—must carry on.

This struggle is about America's message. If you are debating someone and you need a reference to make your point, don't give more credit to anyone than you give yourself. Your opinion is valid. It might need some shaping to be more effective, but it is valid. Your task is to do the work necessary to give your voice the strength needed to breathe life into liberty. Once you have done so, there remains only one thing to do: Get out there and speak.

There are ample opportunities for everyone to speak. But these opportunities require that we each step out of our individual comfort zones and into the public square. I encourage everyone to go to meetings in your community. If there are no meetings, then organize them. Get out of your comfort zone and go to work. A frequent excuse for not speaking out is a fear of speaking in public. That's a perfectly natural fear and everyone has it at some point. However, just as our opponents have so recently used fear to stifle the voice of justice and reason in our country, you cannot allow that fear to silence *yours*. There are a myriad of tools available to you to overcome the fear you experience—this book and the ideas it sparks within you being first among them.

It is my fundamental belief that most Americans know, intuitively, that our country is headed in the wrong direction. We are, after all, the best educated population on Earth. Yet, until now, we haven't felt enough of an impetus to speak that which we know is right. That is why, if you have an opinion that you *just know to be right*, now is the time to speak it. If you don't have all the facts, people around you will correct you. It is uncomfortable, but it is the fastest and easiest way for you to become involved and get out of your comfort zone. If we can get this well-educated American brainpower working together, with actual *facts* from the reality-based world and our unifying philosophy of liberty and sacrifice, nothing can stop us.

Once you have discarded your own fears, you will see the world open up in ways that you hadn't imagined before. The act of organizing groups in our communities to speak about current events will let us discover that we're not alone. Not to sound cliché, but "If you organize it, they will come." We need to organize these groups even if we don't agree on all issues. This is important, because if you can show me how to look at issues just a little bit from your perspective, you will have done me a big favor. You will have opened my eyes to possibilities and facets of life I would never have seen before speaking with you.

This is the case simply because no one person has all of the answers. I know I certainly don't have all the answers. I am not Bill O'Reilly or Rush Limbaugh—I know that I don't know everything. I also know that I alone cannot stop the downward spiral in which I find my country trapped. That's why I wrote this book: I want to find the answers by working with other Americans and creating a message of hope and commitment that we can be proud to give to future generations. This isn't about me, or any other individual—it's about the message. It's about your message. It's about *our* message. If we could each share our message with a dozen other people each a year, we could change our country for the better.

Unfortunately, we don't just need to change our country—we need to *save* our country. We have reached a point in our national course where we have to make hard decisions. We have to come together and recognize that we are the ones in charge of this country, and make the collective decision to throw off the yoke of corporate and partisan tyranny hitched around our necks. The responsibility is, and always has been, ours. That is why we don't have time to wait for the conversation to grow at such a slow pace. We need to speak our message to each other *now*. We need to share our ideas with each other *now* to make ourselves stronger and to ensure we are heard. As we develop our own discourse and ideas in our communities, we can understand the issues and together create the arguments to support our positions. America needs *your* voice and ideas now! We need to get the message out that America will not be destroyed from within!

As I noted before, most of the barriers that keep us from the public square are meaningless. However, a lack of experience doesn't prevent you from asking questions. You see, it really doesn't matter how old or young you are. You could be voting for the fist time in 2008 or someone who cast his first vote in 1912. You have an opinion that is vital to the survival of this nation—simply by virtue of being an American. It is your duty for the wellbeing of all to speak it. We have to begin the dialogue now—one conversation at a time, one American to another.

Right now you are probably asking: "What does it matter if I speak to my neighbors? Everything seems to be going fairly well for me right now. I've got my car(s) and a 37" HDTV. I've got a house in a suburban neighborhood without sidewalks, my kids are bussing off miles to school everyday, I'm swimming in minimum credit card payments, and the house payment is going to break my ARM soon. Life is good, right? Or at least if life isn't good, it's not so bad, and right now I don't have time to worry about anything but the above".

Have you paused to take stock of this situation? Have you ever asked yourself: How did I get here? Why don't I know my neighbors or talk to them regularly? It is simple enough to understand what has happened. We've been distracted by the big screen, projecting infotainment at us. We have been lulled into a false comfort zone. And our "leaders" have worked to achieve that. We live to consume, our Consumer in Chief has admonished us to "Go about your life" in the face of terrorism. Continue to shop, and to buy houses, and play video games. CONSUME! That is all you have to do, and America will be great. This is that false comfort zone they have created for us to defend. Our leaders, for the most part, need us to be caught up in our personal lives of consumption as a distraction. This way, we won't notice as the world crumbles around us. If we don't wake up and start seeing the world around us as it actually is—and what it is becoming—it will be too late to turn it around. Right now it's not too late, but time is running out. The ultimate end result we must seek is to make our public servants actually *serve the public interest.*

In addition to the distractions foisted upon us in the media, there is the constant state of fear in which we have lived since the attacks of 2001. Let's talk about that fear. If our leaders are prone to fear—and prone to use fear against us—the question we must ask ourselves, since those leading us have demonstrated themselves to be cowards: Does the government reflect the make up of the people, or do the people reflect the government? Since we are self-governed, it has to be one or the other; there can be no other explanation. Given this fact, it is time for Americans to engage in some serious, and undoubtedly painful, self examination.

An examination of our American character is in order, both on a national and an individual level. Because our leaders represent us—at least in theory—the first part of our national self examination is this question: Are we proud to be led by cowards? The embarrassing truth, whether we want to admit it or not, is that our leaders *are* cowards. We need to face up to this fact not for our own sakes alone, but rather for our soldiers'. American soldiers are dying half way around the world in defense of our homeland.

They are over there to protect our freedoms, which "they" (the terrorists) hate so much. And how have our cowardly politicians chosen to protect that which our soldiers are dying to defend? By destroying the very freedoms our country's best and brightest have sworn and died to protect.

*   *   *   *

Paging Alanis Morissette! Apparently we are witnessing the death of both liberty *and* irony in America today. When our politicians—or "leaders" (please read the word leaders with as much of a sneer as possible in the narrative voice inside your head)—claim that we must destroy our liberties to save them—from nothing more than fear, or so it would seem—they are speaking for us. Our cowards' betrayal of this country's foundational liberties is the starkest proof that they—Congress and this president—don't really support the troops, don't really support the people, and certainly don't support the Constitution.

You see, it takes more than money and words to support the troops: It takes a commitment to the preservation of our national principles—against all enemies. And yet, do you believe our cowards are committed to the principles contained in our Bill of Rights? I don't believe they are. And I have observed that most Americans don't believe so either. Our cowards, they talk a really good game—that's a politician's job—but when it comes to action, they scamper away and hide—frightened rats whose sewer-home has just been disturbed.

I hope you noticed the use of the phrase "our cowards" because that is at the crux of the first part of the painful self examination we are undertaking here. We have to own these cowards, because they are our own. We elected them, and continue to elect them, and as long as we go on doing so, we will continue to have cowards to lead us. There are many arguments about why we are always stuck with the same mediocre or poor leadership, but ultimately the responsibility lies with us for their actions.

Representative democracy works well when those being governed are informed *and* involved. As I noted before briefly, our cowards have hidden liberty's light behind a veil of secrecy. This is one way in which we have been led off track. Our president tries to classify everything as top secret, and we have a rogue 4th branch of the government in the vice president that seeks to make up his own "Top Secret" status for documents. In fact this Administration's penchant for secrecy is so well known, any further discussion of that here would be redundant. The point is: Our cowards have kept hidden the information that we need to make sure we are governing ourselves correctly. Add to this their constant partisan schemes for congressional redistricting, which ensure that their seats are "safe", and it's no wonder we don't know what's going on—and have no say in it.

By keeping us in the dark and ensuring their continued safe reelections, our cowards have set up a system, with our apathetic consent, in which we have essentially outsourced our responsibility for governance to D.C. Just as large corporations outsource technical support calls to India. It is this system of deferred and distant responsibility, coupled with a constant front of obfuscation and secrecy, which allows the abuses that we see to continue. The abuses of which I speak are not restricted to the war alone, but are certainly illustrative of the situation in which we find ourselves. Let me list a few of those abuses here to drive the point home. The easiest example are the billions of dollars in *no-bid* contracts for services for everything from feeding the troops to guarding U.S. diplomats, all issued during the course of this war. The employment and use of a private mercenary army and an army of contractors that rivals the size of our active duty combat personnel also illustrates the abuse. Finally, Congress' culpability is most notable by the utter lack of oversight committee hearings on war funding for the great bulk of this conflict. No one has been watching the people's purse in the people's House as they've all been too busy helping their buddies cash in on the war at the taxpayers' expense.

Now that we have come to a brief understanding of our leaders' fault, it is time for us to begin the second part of that painful self-examination. In order to do this we need each answer only this one question: Am I afraid? Arguably most of us are, and for good reason. Our cowards have been leading us down a path of darkness for the better part of a decade now, ever since the attacks that they shamelessly used to gain political advantage. In light of all of this, it is vital that we each understand this fact: There's no shame in being afraid. Fear is a natural response to danger, yet the measure is how you react to it. The soldiers that we are asking to fight and die for us experience fear under fire. However, our soldiers do their duty, swallow their fear, and complete their mission everyday. What are

Americans doing at home? Are we doing our duty to protect our liberties, or do we expect others to do it? We have a Congress that appeases those who use fear as a weapon, so we cannot count on them to protect us.

Since we cannot rely on our cowards to lead us out of fear, we then must look elsewhere for a means of extracting ourselves from the darkness. Fortunately, just as we need look no further than our bathroom mirrors to see the root cause of our current state, so too is the solution staring back at us. The first thing we need to do, as I have already discussed throughout this chapter, is to speak to each other and prove to one another this important point: The free and constant exercise of our liberties is the *only* way to guarantee that they endure.

In speaking with people since I returned from Iraq, I have had many conversations about how America *used* to be a community. Almost everyone says that we need to rediscover that quality. In one conversation, someone expressed to me that she felt that community came from the top down—that it required leadership. While I can see her point of view on this, I must respectfully disagree. In a country with actual leaders, maybe we could turn to government to provide a guide to achieve the community we desire. But we don't have actual leaders in America right now. They have proven themselves, time and again, to be complete lickspittle. They complain so often that they don't have the votes to take action. Next time you get the chance to ask a politician a question (which for most of us is never), ask him this: "If you can't muster the votes to pass legislation, why should I vote for you when it is your job to persuade others and you keep failing to do so?"

Believe me, politicians are not ready for people to question their leadership abilities. And when they stumble to give an answer to that question you will have all the proof that you need to conclude that they are not leaders. Therefore, we must turn to each other for that leadership. It is in our neighborhoods that we actually find community and create the leaders we need to begin to rebuild what has been destroyed in the name of short term profits for the well-connected.

Turning to our neighbors is the beginning of what is often called grassroots change. I prefer to call it *citizenship*. We are a self-governing Republic, so we are required to govern: We must make our government answer to our will.

If we just keep doing as we have been doing, turning to Washington, DC for the answers, we will soon experience a shocking defeat and the loss of our individual freedoms. Remember, there is only one power on Earth strong enough to defeat us—ourselves. We have handed that power over wholesale to a government that believes it has no responsibility to us and is actually waging war against us.

There are some that may call this alarmist, but those people would have called Paul Revere's ride alarmist. What I see happening is just as real as a column of Red Coats on the march. Our current governmental climate reminds me very much of the intolerable situation which inspired the founders to create and publish the Declaration of Independence. Talk about getting out of your comfort zone! They specifically knew how far they had gone, to the point of stating explicitly at the end of it: "We mutually pledge to each other our lives, our fortunes and our sacred honor". They understood that by declaring their government corrupt, illegitimate and irrelevant to their lives, they were declaring themselves traitors to their king (i.e. "government"). But to us, they were patriots.

After throwing off the British yoke of tyranny, the founders debated and created our Constitution. There is a reason that they chose to specifically protect free speech in the First Amendment. It seems that our founders knew that ability to freely speak out was the key to a thriving democracy. Therefore, as we combat the cowards that are terrorizing us at every turn by using the mechanisms of our own government, we must keep shouting from the rooftops. By constantly doing this, the powers-that-be would have less chance to silence us. This works because the more noise you make, the more attention a forced silence would generate. This government is rightfully—and ought to be—afraid of making First Amendment martyrs. Therefore, to remain free and safe from the oppressive techniques of your government, you must keep speaking out. It will prove to be your only protection.

Yes, our government would prefer that we remain silent. So much so, that they create "Free Speech Zones" for those who disagree with public officials when they make public speeches on public property to "public" audiences. But it is our duty to remind them that the *whole country* is a free speech zone and take back what they have robbed from us: Our liberty and our collective honor.

Our Congress is crippled with fear over how they will be perceived if something bad happens and the president can point to them and say, "See?! If they had given me everything I wanted, this wouldn't have happened." The cowards are so petrified of the 30 second hatchet ad back home, that they can't do the job that they were elected to do. Though why we are surprised by this behavior should really be the surprise here. Our cowards are so focused on reelection they are incapable of leading. So it should be no revelation that words alone strike the greatest chords of fear in their hearts. Therefore, we must make sure that they understand that we already know them by their actions—and their votes against liberty are the strongest facts that prove their infidelity to us and to our future.

Throughout this book, I have tried to make one inescapable point: Our current situation is the result of fear perpetuated by a cowardly and inertia-laden leadership. Because of this, we must find a solution to our fear. The answer is obvious: If you *don't* fear the government, it is time to stand up and say "*Enough!*" If you *do* fear the government, it is time to stand up and say "*Stop!*" We have been afraid too long and we have reached a time when we can no longer allow fear to get in our way. Our homeland is at stake. We are on the verge of losing our Republic. This not an exaggeration, I am completely and undeniably serious about this.

If you don't think that putting an end to the erosion of our Constitution is a big deal, just remember that serfdom comes next. If you don't know what serfdom is, I will not explain it. It is serious enough for you to take the time to look it up—because *you* will be the one suffering under the yoke of a corporate master, with no recourse at law. This is what's next for us if we just sit back and let things unfold. Those that want to take your rights already have their hands on the levers of power. We have—for now—the power to wrest those levers from our cowards' greedy and grasping hands.

However, time is limited. I fervently believe that we are at a true crisis point now that will come to a head within the next few congressional election cycles. Failure to act within this timeframe will most likely mean that it will be too late. This book is my first proof that I will be silent no longer. It is past time for the government to fear the people—they must know that they will be held accountable; and the laws they create to protect themselves from being tried for their crimes in our courts of justice will not stand. This must be a key demand that we, as citizens exercising our liberties in order to defend them, make of our leaders in this and subsequent elections. The disastrous laws enacted by our most recent crops of cowards must be repealed. The rule of law must be reinstated as the primary governing principle for our country. We must make it clear to those who hold and will seek office that appeasers and facilitators of this overt treason will be held accountable.

Ultimately it comes down to facing our fear as the only defense against the further loss of our liberties, and the only hope of recapturing those already lost. I can only tell you that I have faced my fear. I find it ironic that I learned to face my fears in a combat zone, put there as a soldier by the very government that is trying to frighten me at home. After facing my fear of death, there isn't much else that anyone can do to frighten me. That is part of the reason why I am not afraid of my government today. That is probably also why so many war veterans march and speak at war protests. We have all come, through different paths, to understand that *dissent is patriotic*. After my war experiences, I would be ashamed to admit to myself that I fear the cowards running my government. My experiences in Iraq, and what I've witnessed upon my return to the States, tell me that a cabal of cowards, who send other people to war, while insisting that their families should not go, at the same time living fat off the work of others' successes, as they give away our collective wealth to their cronies, are nothing to cause any fear.

It is true that terrorists killed more than three thousand Americans on 9/11. We must now decide if we will betray our liberties in their name. Do we fear to walk down the street because of what has happened before? Do we hand over our rights to a government we know does not concern itself with our collective best interest? Is that the right answer: We just buckle under and give up because a few terrorists got lucky? That's what our government wants us to do. And our Congress, the last hope of keeping our Republic alive, caves in out of fear.

Those are our "leaders". We are led by fearful men. Let's give them something to fear. How can we do that? What power do we have? Take to the streets! Speak out!

You may feel that, as one person, you can't make enough of a difference to bother with becoming engaged in government, politics, or even the community. But let me help you a little bit: When all of the wrongs committed by our current government come to light in the years ahead, you will not be allowed to claim ignorance. It is irrelevant that you have been kept in the dark by the government's claims that they needed to keep so many things secret. They are doing it in your name. The world refused to allow German society to claim ignorance of the Holocaust after World War II, and we will be shown no more mercy than they were shown.

When the light of day shines upon these crimes being committed in your name, you will be held responsible. You will be the one to hang your head in shame and have to admit that it was done on your behalf. You will be guilty. We cannot go back and undo what has already been done, but we can stop the continuation of these evils done in our name. In order to do that, we are required to hold those directly responsible for enacting these evils accountable to us. Since we, collectively, will be held blameworthy by future generations, it is in our best interest—and theirs—that we hold these criminals responsible before history places an indelible black mark on our time.

Now that I have called out our so-called leaders on their cowardice and betrayal, I want to address how they can redeem themselves. But we have to go back and ask, once again, these important questions: What is America about? How far should we go to protect our Constitution? Should we defend it to the last man or should we, at some point, say that it's just not worth it and abandon it?

These are important questions. How far do we go? Is it time to just accept that terrorists have defeated us and we should scrap our checks and balances in favor of a single, absolute ruler? Or should we defend our Republic against all attacks, even those from within? Should we abandon the system and individual liberties the framers shaped into our Constitution in favor of an unchecked government with absolute power?

These are the questions that face us today. Even if you don't like politics, these decisions affect you. If the government needs authority to combat terrorism that is specifically denied in the Constitution, then should we amend the document to give it to them? Or should we just let them whittle away at the document through unconstitutional laws that are recognized by a partisan court system, thereby destroying it from within?

I have to admit that I hope what I am writing makes you uncomfortable, afraid, or angry. Because those emotions are the basis of the motivation you will need to leave your favorite chair in front of your TV, get out of your comfort zone, and become involved in your government.

In speaking with people about the state of our country, I find the anger to be palpable. You can feel it in the air. But my perception is that the anger isn't so much over what is being done (or the lack of it), it's more due to the desperate feeling that the people are being ignored. There's no other explanation for it—Congress caves in on every issue embraced by the go-it-alone-my-way-or-the-high-way president and they become unpopular for not having the conviction of their rhetoric, and their approval numbers spiral downward faster than those of the president. It's because they were expected to do something about these dead-end state of affairs.

This anger that I perceive in the population isn't confined to the Left or Right, Democrat or Republican. It's anger at being ignored. Keep in mind that I live in Utah, so as a liberal I have a very small audience. But people nonetheless talk with me because of my status as an Iraq war veteran. Most people haven't seen Iraq, and they will listen and ask questions of returning veterans. I am not ashamed of using this status to achieve my personal soap box. But I have seen politicians who have never served in uniform exploit the military for their own political purposes, so I have no problem with exploiting my experiences to get this message out.

From these conversations, I find that people from across the political spectrum agree on the fact that America is definitely careening down the wrong track. But everyone arrives at this conclusion from a different place on the political spectrum. How can it be that people who see only red or blue can arrive at the same conclusion? It's simple: Most Americans don't see only red or blue. They see *red, white, and blue*. Nonetheless, most people have a particular political bent, so, again, how can they arrive at the same conclusion independently? The answer to that is also simple: Politics is not a linear spectrum, it is a continuum. Left folds into right and vice versa. A liberal of today was a conservative of the past, and a conservative of today fought the liberal revolutions of yesterday.

The reality is that the political labels we choose to accept for ourselves—or to throw at our opponents—are irrelevant. For example, those true conservatives (i.e. those that are actually committed to the Constitution) have allowed George W. Bush to drape himself in that word, like George Costanza drapes himself in velvet whenever possible. That means the word can no longer be used to describe those actual conservatives; Bush has sullied the word to the point of incompatibility with its traditional meaning. So how can a conservative continue to use the word effectively—and properly—when the meaning of the word has been co-opted by someone who is far from the philosophy underpinning the actual meaning of that word?

But conservatives might take little comfort in knowing that they are not alone. Liberals have accepted the disdain of the opposing political hacks and surrendered the noble intentions of liberalism to the often violent radical Left. I use these points to illustrate that both "sides" of this spectrum have skeletons in our closets. But, more importantly, there are no *sides*: We are all part of the same traditions of freedom and the labels are irrelevant.

In conversation, if we accept these labels of liberal or conservative as our own, we may distance ourselves from others because of their preconceived notions due to the recent misapplication of those words. In America, as contradictory as it sounds, true liberals and true conservatives are actually very close to each other on the fundamental questions. Therefore, everyone should shun these labels. When speaking to other people, don't brand your opinions by which part of the "spectrum" you believe you used to arrive at your position, instead ignore the label and speak as an *American*. After that, you can apply any label you want. And then each side can begin the fight to retake the meanings of their own words, conservative and liberal.

Our Constitution came out of the fight against tyranny. And by definition, only liberals fight revolutions. Out of that liberal struggle, we founded a nation. And by defending it, those ideals became conservative. But they have never lost their liberal zeal.

One friend of mine told me that he didn't agree with half the stuff I said about most things, but when it came to my opinions about the state of our government, he agreed almost 100%. Here he is a conservative (he went out of his way to point out that conservative to him didn't equate to Republican), and because of what was being done in the United States today, he felt the time is near to move to Idaho and start a compound like Randy Weaver's at Ruby Ridge. Of course, he was just being dramatic, but you get the point. The crux of his anger was directed at the loss of civil liberties in this country. He rightly recognized that it all boils down to that. Without our liberties, we have nothing. And they *are* worth fighting for.

This interaction illustrates my point that it isn't hard to notice the anger all around you. People have lost trust in their government, and they are angry about this. But that anger stems from the fear of losing hope in their future. The solution to our current problems can be found in the past—the struggle for and preservation of our liberties. We are in that struggle together. It doesn't matter what our individual philosophies are or how we arrived at them, we all have the same goals: Life, liberty and the pursuit of happiness. Life is worthless without liberty and you will never find happiness under oppression.

President Bush has complained that people who oppose his overall policies forget that we are at war. As if being the Commander-in-Chief means he should never be questioned. He counts on that kind of deference; otherwise he would have nothing else to command respect. However, his assertion that others have forgotten that we are at war could not be more mistaken. No one has forgotten that we are at war, but it is quite obvious that this president has forgotten *what we are fighting for*.

If you are afraid enough, and angry enough, you are ready for the last emotion needed: Resolve. I want to do what I can to help you get you out of your comfort zone and take part in the noble fight for our country. My only hope to do that is to help you to understand the problems that urgently demand our collective attention. The crux of those problems lies squarely with our "leadership". It is time for a serious change, and you can effect that change through your action—speaking with neighbors, going to public meetings, or doing anything that gets your concerns heard by others. This will create that which we most need: Community.

There is in important reason for Americans to once again band together to force much needed change. As you may have noticed, government decisions swing back and forth between Left and Right. This is natural and happens in every country that is self-governed by the people. It's like a pendulum swinging back and forth. You may have also noticed that America is currently being artificially restricted from this natural movement by a radical Far-Right agenda. Everything from stem cell research to health care coverage for lower-middle-class children are being restricted due to the artificial "morality" of a few zealots, demanding that we all live as they dictate.

Congress keeps complaining that they don't have the votes to pass anything with enough support to override a presidential veto. As I said before, it is important to recognize that if a politician can't persuade—an important part of a politician's job—they are of no use to us. In fact, they harm our national security and interests through their incompetence. This failure of personal leadership on their part is inexcusable and unacceptable. Public opinion has strongly turned against the radical Right wing, but we are unable to do anything to enforce our desired change because there are too many smirking cowards in Congress.

Americans are accustomed to rapid change. We like to have our new technology delivered *yesterday*. Some people even camp out waiting to pay top dollar for the latest gadget. This demand for instant gratification probably stems from our heritage. Think about it, if the founders hadn't been impatient for changes in representation in governance, they probably wouldn't have begun the fight for independence. Our individual desire for the next innovation is a direct result of this tradition.

Collectively, I believe that we can conclude that lack of rapid change equals radical change. There are two dangers from this situation: Either people will overreact and cause harm or become apathetic and fail to act. Either way, our desire for change is good, but the manner in which we choose to demand that change matters as well. At this point, though, I believe the greater harm would be from us not acting for the changes we all see are needed. The cowardly Congress won't do as we instructed them in the 2006 midterm elections, so we have to turn elsewhere: Ourselves. Getting all Americans out of their comfort zone now will prevent any harm that could result from a rapid backlash against the Far Right.

But I don't believe we are in danger of overreacting to what is happening. No. I believe the biggest danger we face is from allowing an artificial constraint against needed change to retain dominance. And the root of that danger is that we will, as we have demonstrated so many times before, become apathetic. Because we have no patience to wait for the desired change, and since our government has many times before simply waited us out, we may just grow weary of the fight and let them take what they want.

The Neoconservatives who have taken our country to the brink of the disaster on which it now teeters were very patient—it took them decades to attain the power they have been wielding against We the People like a club. We must adopt the same deliberate tenacity they demonstrated while planning their coup, but we don't have the luxury of hiding in ivory towers developing morally bankrupt policies with intellectually dishonest rhetoric. We simply *don't have the time.* Truth is both our shield and sword against their lies. And if we can prove the resolve of the American people to retake our country in our own name, we won't have to wait for nearly half a century as they did. If it comes down to requiring decades to fix what has already been done to us, we must begin that clean up process now. We don't have time to hope that it works itself out.

With regard to the policies that we desperately need to change—those dealing with fundamental rights that can be asserted against government intrusion—we cannot act fast enough. As long as we look to the Constitution for guidance, it will be impossible to overreach. The powers that the Bush Administration has seized, with the acquiescence of a pliable, opportunistic Congress, are the radical end result of the pendulum swinging too far to the Right.

A progressive voice is not heard in this country today. That's not to say there isn't a progressive voice—because there is. It is simply not heard today because of the static coming from the Far Right trying to muddy the waters in order to obscure the fact that they have no new ideas other than hate and oppression. The Left is devoid of substance because anger has replaced rational thought. I know because I am a liberal and I have felt that anger, but I have replaced it with resolve. Resolve is the natural progression after anger—after you realize that anger itself will not solve the problems. Action is required.

I use the pendulum as an illustration, but keep in mind my earlier assertion that our political spectrum is more akin to a continuum—the American philosophy of governance is all part of the same fabric.

I have said before in these pages that Americans are *supposed* to be the good guys. That's because we know ourselves to actually *be* the good guys. It is time for us to start *acting* like it again. The solution for most of our pressing problems, economic *and* national security is to become a community again. But it doesn't stop there. We must be vigilant against those we place in government who often become drunk on the power we entrust them with, and obstinate in their belief of personal infallibility.

Many people can rightfully claim that they are already involved in their community through their church or other social organization. For those, I say don't stop reading—there is more still to do.

The fact that America has been the melting pot of the world for over a century proves our commitment to tolerance of those who are different. I know that we have an ugly history of intolerance, but that has mostly been due to the ignorance that our government has foisted upon us through their unconscionable policies and laws. We can no longer claim ignorance. In this age of high speed information flow, virtually everyone has the means to learn the truth. And the truth is that we are more than a community, we are a family. And always have been. It is for each individual to find this truth for himself, and the best way to find that truth is through community participation.

For those of you actively involved in a church or other social group, it is your responsibility to convince the others in your group to be all-inclusive. We cannot exclude people on blind prejudice. Try to remember that we are all Americans. Yes, even undocumented workers are Americans. They might not be citizens, but America is an *idea* that calls to the heart of all freedom loving people. And America, by having the reputation around the world of being the land of opportunity, will keep calling to them. It is far too convenient to give in to the rhetoric of those currently in power, who try to blame our problems on immigrants, gays, and anyone different from themselves. The blame rightly belongs with all of us and we have to work together to find the solutions—and we have to draw on every resource we have. It will take a great deal of hard work and no one willing to shoulder some of the burden should be excluded.

Politicians are expert at throwing red herrings in the face of the public to divert focus from their wrongdoing. They will respond to public concerns about particular important issues, but they will blame immigrants or other identifiable groups and then, after successfully distracting your attention, they are free to ignore the underlying issues that caused your concerns in the first place. These smelly-fish methods are not always easy to identify, but they can be avoided by remaining true to our philosophy—always ask yourself, "Does what this politician is saying address the actual problem at hand?" When a politician is speaking, you will most often answer that question in the negative, and then you will know that you are dealing with a red herring. A direct way to identify if a legislative bill is valid to the issue is to ask, "Does this proposal ensure domestic tranquility, provide for the common defense, promote the general welfare, or advance the effort to secure the blessings of liberty?" If not, then it is not worth our acceptance.

*　　　*　　　*　　　*

After re-establishing ourselves within our local communities, those communities need to begin to communicate amongst themselves. There are many methods available for this. Leaders of the community-groups need to step up and find the methods most suitable for your group (remember, everyone in a community group should strive to be a leader at some point—this country is in dire need of leadership today and we need everyone to develop those skills, we don't know what tomorrow may bring and any one of us could be called upon to shoulder the burdens of leadership at any time).

Once the community groups have begun to communicate (but don't wait for that to be complete, all of these methods can be implemented simultaneously), those groups must approach government officials to redress grievances. It is a constitutional right of the people to do this, but with the exception of well-paid legislative lobbyists (at the state and federal levels), few of us are able to exercise it. We must rectify this situation.

George W. Bush, after his actual election by national majority vote in 2004, stated bluntly that, "The accountability moment is over." Not so much. Every government official, elected or appointed, at all levels, is constantly accountable to us. We must remind them of this fact. Right now, they are most fearful of the monied interests that can withhold funding for their campaigns. We must make them understand that they have misplaced their fear: They need to fear *us*. We have entrusted in them our future, and they have betrayed that trust. It is time they understand that we hold their futures in our hands and they will not escape retribution for their infidelity.

Mere petitions won't do. We each need to make a commitment in our community groups to *visit* our local politicians. Not all at once, but continually—and repeatedly. You see, writing letters and signing petitions is too easy. These politicians don't respond to requests unless there is a large sum of money attached to support their re-election efforts. They have control of the system and they like it this way. They are corrupt. Period. But if a constant stream of people visits their office, they *have* to take notice. People that are willing to get out of their comfort zones to confront politicians make those politicians very uncomfortable and nervous. Because they know that people who will take action will not be satisfied with words. And such people can gain influence in their communities. This they fear. And they have proven with their recent votes that fear is the only thing they understand. Let's give them something to fear—us.

With enough people behind our local and national community efforts, the politicians will soon realize where the power is and always has been—with us. When we once again prove that they have reason to fear us, they will respond.

I can feel all around me that the American people are desperate for an actual leader. I can also feel that Americans want to come together and solve the problems facing us. But they don't know how. Besides my personal perceptions of this all around me, I have heard people voice these very sentiments. The solution is simple. It's the implementation of that solution that's hard. Everyone knows that we have to come together in an era of shared sacrifice, and most Americans at this time are ready to do just that. But they don't have a leader with the conviction or strength to develop a plan or even to ask for the needed sacrifice.

Don't confuse sacrifice with deprivation. We don't need to ration food like during World War II. We just need to be careful in the use of our collective national and natural resources, from defense to the use of fossil fuels. I have not been elected to any office, nor do I seek election; I am just a concerned American. So, since we don't have any elected leaders left in this country, I will take the first step and ask you to join me. Come with me and take that first individual step toward our collective sacrifice which will lead us back to prosperity, liberty, and justice.

Since I am asking you to step out of your comfort zone, and become engaged in public discourse, I need to arm you against the attacks you will inevitably face from those that disagree with you. The most common type of argument that opponents will retreat to is to attack you for who you are. It is important that you are able to recognize this for what it is when you see it.

These are known as ad hominem attacks. You will recognize these by the fact that they do not address the issue at hand, but instead address some irrelevancy (most probably about you personally, in the attempt to diminish your credibility or to distract you from your line of reasoning). All you have to do is ask yourself, "Does this address what we're talking about?" If the answer is no, point out his red herring and force him back to the issue. Just remember that a person who employs an ad hominem implicitly accepts your side of things (because they don't have a counter argument), and you should take advantage of that.

People prone to use ad hominem attacks are also prone to attempt to frame the debate by using certain words with popularly-accepted meanings. As an example, such people often use the word "conservative" as a shield, as if that word alone gives them some sort of moral authority over every subject. But as I have discussed in this chapter, conservative and liberal are part of the same political spectrum, they fold into each other. Not everyone is purely conservative or liberal; those labels are actually beside the point. If someone attempts to use a label, such as "conservative", for themselves in order to use the "liberal" label against you, you need to ask them this direct question: "What branch of the U.S. military did you serve in?" When they say they didn't serve (which is most likely the answer you will receive), point out that true conservatives defend their country with their lives, not their words, and then direct the discussion back to the original point.

Let me give you a personal example. When someone speaks with me about Iraq, I try to make it perfectly clear that I do not support the war. And I understand that as a veteran, that holds a little weight with people. One day, I was having lunch in a group, and being an Iraq war vet, people were asking me about it. I was answering their questions and leading them back to the concept of this book, shared sacrifice. One person walked into the room in the middle of the conversation and said, "The problem with "liberals" is they don't understand the war". I bit my tongue as much as I could and pointed out that there are so many chicken-hawk "conservatives" who have never worn a uniform that nonetheless support the war, but don't understand the military. That person was trying to gain credibility by simply using the word "liberal" to distract from the points I was trying to make. And you will note that I didn't let him get away with it.

The point I want you to take from this, dear reader, is that you need to address the assumptions that someone makes about themselves when they take a label such as "conservative" and use it as a shield. You cannot simply accept their world view, you have to confront it. Otherwise, they will use whatever context they choose to pigeon-hole you into implicitly accepting their arguments. Don't fall for this tactic.

Because of our natural discomfiture with public speaking, it will take heart and conviction for you to stand up in a room with several hundred people and speak your mind. But freedom is not free. You will have to make sacrifices. Those sacrifices will require that you accept responsibility for your government's mistakes. But most importantly, those sacrifices will require you to take action. And those actions will require the resolve to do what is necessary for the defense and betterment of your neighborhood, community, and country.

It would be impossible for me to act if I didn't have the ever-optimistic belief that our system has the flexibility to self-correct. The drafters of the Constitution were wise and included that idea in the system they designed. But the words "self-correction" can be misleading: They can cause some people to believe that it will just sort itself out. But that isn't the case. Self-correction means that we must correct it *ourselves*, it will not just work itself out—not without the concerted effort of every American.

I hope that I have been able to communicate to you that I am just as angry as anyone else about what is being done to my country. I know that, despite the words that come out of our politicians' mouths, they are not preserving our cherished traditions. They are instead preoccupied with conveying wealth to their cronies, amassing power for themselves, and experimenting with unproven theories of law and the application of military power to solve diplomatic problems.

But my anger has turned to resolve. I am no longer willing to just sit at home and fume over what is being done in my name. I intend to take action. This book is only the first of what for me will be a lifetime of active involvement. I hope you will join me. We need every American to act if we are going to recapture our national honor and legitimacy—and once again become the beacon of freedom our country was founded to be.

I hope everyone recognizes that it is up to each of us—yes, even *you*—to take back our country. I can write a book and scream at the top of my lungs, but unless we all get out of our comfort zones and actually take action, nothing will get done. We owe it to the future to act *now* to make the world a better place for those yet born. Imagine where we would be today if everyone in Lexington had just slept through Paul Revere's ride.

AFTERWORD

I am new to the world of mass communications and activism, but I am definitely here to stay. To that end, I have set up a website which I intend to be an information clearinghouse for patriotic activism directed toward taking back our country. The website has a blog for people to post information or ideas for the benefit of all concerned Americans. I will produce and post on the site a regular podcast to keep information flowing and to continue the uniquely American experience of Shared Sacrifice. The address is:

www.sharedsacrifice.us

We need all Americans to rise to the defense of our country. And if you are a veteran, your country especially needs you again. You need to stand up and be heard—*now*. What position you take isn't the issue, it is important that you speak. In the current environment, veterans must suit up and do our duty once again. I know, you've already answered the call once (or more), what more can be expected of you? That depends on you! You need to be heard. We veterans have been exploited far too long. Those in power use a lot of words to praise us in order to support the war, but their actions of betrayal after we come home speak for themselves. We have a voice in this and we need to use it or others will suffer. I'm sure every veteran recognizes that we have a duty to our country that can *never* be completely fulfilled. We owe it to the future. We all can be proud to say we have fought for freedom before. Sadly, when rest is well-deserved, we will have to rejoin the fight for our country again—*now*.

At this point, however, I want to make a personal statement to retired general officers. If you are a general who retired during the Global War on Terror era, I don't care what you have to say. If you couldn't stand up and speak truth to power while you were in uniform, *as your duty required*, you have nothing I care to hear. Most retired generals now speak out because it is in vogue—and financially profitable for them—to do so. If they had the faith of their oath to the Constitution, they would have done what was right when it could have made a difference, even if it meant just resigning in protest to demonstrate that they would take no part in the disasters visited upon America through the lies of a Neoconservative cabal. But they were afraid to lose their retirement income, status as a senior officer, or lucrative jobs that their military contacts would get them. My personal message to these former general officers is: "If you couldn't do it while you were in uniform, you missed a vital opportunity and it is now too late for you to gain credibility with veterans like me by speaking out. Your lack of action when it could have made a difference demonstrates your lack of honor and true character better than your words of protest now".

At one of my speaking events, a military retiree who has become an activist with Veterans for Peace (www.veteransforpeace.org), put it perfectly when she said that the government doesn't care about veterans because we have already done our duty—we are *past-tense*. But, like her, all veterans should refuse to be past-tense. We are relevant and must be heard. Let's show those that would relegate us to the dustbin just how relevant we are! We cannot allow another generation of veterans to become forgotten and thrown away by our ungrateful government. Think of the years it took to get adequate body armor for those in harms way, or the Walter Reed Army Hospital outrage, or the fact that a full *quarter* of people living homeless on the streets in America are veterans, and you see what I mean. The government doesn't care about us because they have already used us to our fullest and now they can throw us away. Our choice is simple: We can accept this disloyalty or we can remember that we are the ones who have defended this country in war and we have the strength and honor—and numbers—to force them to respond to us. I'm sorry, my fellow veterans, but there is no time for you to take your well-deserved rest.

*　　　*　　　*　　　*

My late grandfather enlisted underage in the U.S. Navy and sailed during World War I. In tribute to his courage and patriotism, I am proud to share with you a poem he wrote from the home front during World War II:

FLAG OF FOUR FREEDOMS

Freedom from worry, freedom from fear,
Freedom to worship the God you hold dear,
Freedom to govern the land that you own
If you'll but carry, Oh carry me on.

Oh, carry! Oh, carry! Oh carry me on.
Carry me proudly, the flag you have won.
Hoist me up gently and carry me high.
I'll give you freedom as long as I fly.

People of races, color and creed,
All will find safety in believing in me.
Monarchs and tyrants will ne'er own your home,
If you'll but carry, Oh carry me on.

John Arnason
(circa 1945)

APPENDIX A

▼

CONSTITUTION FOR THE UNITED STATES OF AMERICA

Courtesy of the Constitution Society. Retrieved October 25, 2007, from http://www.constitution.org/.

[Constitution for the United States of America]

We the People of the United States, in Order to form a more perfect Union, establish Justice, insure domestic Tranquility, provide for the common defence, promote the general Welfare, and secure the Blessings of Liberty to ourselves and our Posterity, do ordain and establish this Constitution for the United States of America.

Article. I.

Section. 1. All legislative Powers herein granted shall be vested in a Congress of the United States, which shall consist of a Senate and House of Representatives.

Section. 2. The House of Representatives shall be composed of Members chosen every second Year by the People of the several States, and the Electors in each

State shall have the Qualifications requisite for Electors of the most numerous Branch of the State Legislature.

No Person shall be a Representative who shall not have attained to the Age of twenty five Years, and been seven Years a Citizen of the United States, and who shall not, when elected, be an Inhabitant of that State in which he shall be chosen.

Representatives and direct Taxes shall be apportioned among the several States which may be included within this Union, according to their respective Numbers, which shall be determined by adding to the whole Number of free Persons, including those bound to Service for a Term of Years, and excluding Indians not taxed, three fifths of all other Persons. The actual Enumeration shall be made within three Years after the first Meeting of the Congress of the United States, and within every subsequent Term of ten Years, in such Manner as they shall by Law direct. The Number of Representatives shall not exceed one for every thirty Thousand, but each State shall have at Least one Representative; and until such enumeration shall be made, the State of New Hampshire shall be entitled to chuse three, Massachusetts eight, Rhode-Island and Providence Plantations one, Connecticut five, New-York six, New Jersey four, Pennsylvania eight, Delaware one, Maryland six, Virginia ten, North Carolina five, South Carolina five, and Georgia three.

When vacancies happen in the Representation from any State, the Executive Authority thereof shall issue Writs of Election to fill such Vacancies.

The House of Representatives shall chuse their Speaker and other Officers; and shall have the sole Power of Impeachment.

Section. 3. The Senate of the United States shall be composed of two Senators from each State, chosen by the Legislature thereof, for six Years; and each Senator shall have one Vote.
Immediately after they shall be assembled in Consequence of the first Election, they shall be divided as equally as may be into three Classes. The Seats of the Senators of the first Class shall be vacated at the Expiration of the second Year, of the second Class at the Expiration of the fourth Year, and of the third Class at the Expiration of the sixth Year, so that one third may be chosen every second Year; and if Vacancies happen by Resignation, or otherwise, during the Recess of the

Legislature of any State, the Executive thereof may make temporary Appointments until the next Meeting of the Legislature, which shall then fill such Vacancies.

No Person shall be a Senator who shall not have attained to the Age of thirty Years, and been nine Years a Citizen of the United States, and who shall not, when elected, be an Inhabitant of that State for which he shall be chosen.

The Vice President of the United States shall be President of the Senate, but shall have no Vote, unless they be equally divided.

The Senate shall chuse their other Officers, and also a President pro tempore, in the Absence of the Vice President, or when he shall exercise the Office of President of the United States.

The Senate shall have the sole Power to try all Impeachments. When sitting for that Purpose, they shall be on Oath or Affirmation. When the President of the United States is tried, the Chief Justice shall preside: And no Person shall be convicted without the Concurrence of two thirds of the Members present.

Judgment in Cases of Impeachment shall not extend further than to removal from Office, and disqualification to hold and enjoy any Office of honor, Trust or Profit under the United States: but the Party convicted shall nevertheless be liable and subject to Indictment, Trial, Judgment and Punishment, according to Law.

Section. 4. The Times, Places and Manner of holding Elections for Senators and Representatives, shall be prescribed in each State by the Legislature thereof; but the Congress may at any time by Law make or alter such Regulations, except as to the Places of chusing Senators.

The Congress shall assemble at least once in every Year, and such Meeting shall be on the first Monday in December, unless they shall by Law appoint a different Day.

Section. 5. Each House shall be the Judge of the Elections, Returns and Qualifications of its own Members, and a Majority of each shall constitute a Quorum to do Business; but a smaller Number may adjourn from day to day, and may be authorized to compel the Attendance of absent Members, in such Manner, and under such Penalties as each House may provide.

Each House may determine the Rules of its Proceedings, punish its Members for disorderly Behaviour, and, with the Concurrence of two thirds, expel a Member. Each House shall keep a Journal of its Proceedings, and from time to time publish the same, excepting such Parts as may in their Judgment require Secrecy; and the Yeas and Nays of the Members of either House on any question shall, at the Desire of one fifth of those Present, be entered on the Journal.

Neither House, during the Session of Congress, shall, without the Consent of the other, adjourn for more than three days, nor to any other Place than that in which the two Houses shall be sitting.

Section. 6. The Senators and Representatives shall receive a Compensation for their Services, to be ascertained by Law, and paid out of the Treasury of the United States. They shall in all Cases, except Treason, Felony and Breach of the Peace, be privileged from Arrest during their Attendance at the Session of their respective Houses, and in going to and returning from the same; and for any Speech or Debate in either House, they shall not be questioned in any other Place.

No Senator or Representative shall, during the Time for which he was elected, be appointed to any civil Office under the Authority of the United States, which shall have been created, or the Emoluments whereof shall have been encreased during such time; and no Person holding any Office under the United States, shall be a Member of either House during his Continuance in Office.

Section. 7. All Bills for raising Revenue shall originate in the House of Representatives; but the Senate may propose or concur with Amendments as on other Bills.
Every Bill which shall have passed the House of Representatives and the Senate, shall, before it become a Law, be presented to the President of the United States; If he approve he shall sign it, but if not he shall return it, with his Objections to that House in which it shall have originated, who shall enter the Objections at large on their Journal, and proceed to reconsider it. If after such Reconsideration two thirds of that House shall agree to pass the Bill, it shall be sent, together with the Objections, to the other House, by which it shall likewise be reconsidered,

and if approved by two thirds of that House, it shall become a Law. But in all such Cases the Votes of both Houses shall be determined by yeas and Nays, and the Names of the Persons voting for and against the Bill shall be entered on the Journal of each House respectively. If any Bill shall not be returned by the President within ten Days (Sundays excepted) after it shall have been presented to him, the Same shall be a Law, in like Manner as if he had signed it, unless the Congress by their Adjournment prevent its Return, in which Case it shall not be a Law.

Every Order, Resolution, or Vote to which the Concurrence of the Senate and House of Representatives may be necessary (except on a question of Adjournment) shall be presented to the President of the United States; and before the Same shall take Effect, shall be approved by him, or being disapproved by him, shall be repassed by two thirds of the Senate and House of Representatives, according to the Rules and Limitations prescribed in the Case of a Bill.

Section. 8. The Congress shall have Power To lay and collect Taxes, Duties, Imposts and Excises, to pay the Debts and provide for the common Defence and general Welfare of the United States; but all Duties, Imposts and Excises shall be uniform throughout the United States; To borrow Money on the credit of the United States; To regulate Commerce with foreign Nations, and among the several States, and with the Indian Tribes; To establish an uniform Rule of Naturalization, and uniform Laws on the subject of Bankruptcies throughout the United States; To coin Money, regulate the Value thereof, and of foreign Coin, and fix the Standard of Weights and Measures; To provide for the Punishment of counterfeiting the Securities and current Coin of the United States; To establish Post Offices and post Roads; To promote the Progress of Science and useful Arts, by securing for limited Times to Authors and Inventors the exclusive Right to their respective Writings and Discoveries; To constitute Tribunals inferior to the supreme Court; To define and punish Piracies and Felonies committed on the high Seas, and Offences against the Law of Nations; To declare War, grant Letters of Marque and Reprisal, and make Rules concerning Captures on Land and Water; To raise and support Armies, but no Appropriation of Money to that Use shall be for a longer Term than two Years; To provide and maintain a Navy; To make Rules for the Government and Regulation of the land and naval Forces; To provide for calling forth the Militia to execute the Laws of the Union, suppress Insurrections and repel Invasions; To provide for organizing, arming, and disciplining, the Militia, and for governing such Part of them as may be employed in the Service of the United States, reserving to the States respectively, the Appointment of the Officers, and the Authority of training the Militia according to the discipline prescribed by Congress; To exercise exclusive Legislation in all Cases whatsoever, over such District (not exceeding ten Miles square) as may, by Cession of particular States, and the Acceptance of Congress, become the Seat of the Government of the United States, and to exercise like Authority over all Places purchased by the Consent of the Legislature of the State in which the Same shall be, for the Erection of Forts, Magazines, Arsenals, dock-Yards, and other needful Buildings;—And

To make all Laws which shall be necessary and proper for carrying into Execution the foregoing Powers, and all other Powers vested by this Constitution in the Government of the United States, or in any Department or Officer thereof.

Section. 9. The Migration or Importation of such Persons as any of the States now existing shall think proper to admit, shall not be prohibited by the Congress prior to the Year one thousand eight hundred and eight, but a Tax or duty may be imposed on such Importation, not exceeding ten dollars for each Person.

The Privilege of the Writ of Habeas Corpus shall not be suspended, unless when in Cases of Rebellion or Invasion the public Safety may require it.

No Bill of Attainder or ex post facto Law shall be passed.

No Capitation, or other direct, Tax shall be laid, unless in Proportion to the Census or Enumeration herein before directed to be taken.

No Tax or Duty shall be laid on Articles exported from any State.

No Preference shall be given by any Regulation of Commerce or Revenue to the Ports of one State over those of another; nor shall Vessels bound to, or from, one State, be obliged to enter, clear, or pay Duties in another.

No Money shall be drawn from the Treasury, but in Consequence of Appropriations made by Law; and a regular Statement and Account of the Receipts and Expenditures of all public Money shall be published from time to time.

No Title of Nobility shall be granted by the United States: And no Person holding any Office of Profit or Trust under them, shall, without the Consent of the

Congress, accept of any present, Emolument, Office, or Title, of any kind whatever, from any King, Prince, or foreign State.

Section. 10. No State shall enter into any Treaty, Alliance, or Confederation; grant Letters of Marque and Reprisal; coin Money; emit Bills of Credit; make any Thing but gold and silver Coin a Tender in Payment of Debts; pass any Bill of Attainder, ex post facto Law, or Law impairing the Obligation of Contracts, or grant any Title of Nobility.
No State shall, without the Consent of the Congress, lay any Imposts or Duties on Imports or Exports, except what may be absolutely necessary for executing it's inspection Laws; and the net Produce of all Duties and Imposts, laid by any State on Imports or Exports, shall be for the Use of the Treasury of the United States; and all such Laws shall be subject to the Revision and Controul of the Congress.

No State shall, without the Consent of Congress, lay any Duty of Tonnage, keep Troops, or Ships of War in time of Peace, enter into any Agreement or Compact with another State, or with a foreign Power, or engage in War, unless actually invaded, or in such imminent Danger as will not admit of delay.

Article. II.

Section. 1. The executive Power shall be vested in a President of the United States of America. He shall hold his Office during the Term of four Years, and, together with the Vice President, chosen for the same Term, be elected, as follows:

Each State shall appoint, in such Manner as the Legislature thereof may direct, a Number of Electors, equal to the whole Number of Senators and Representatives to which the State may be entitled in the Congress: but no Senator or Representative, or Person holding an Office of Trust or Profit under the United States, shall be appointed an Elector.

The Electors shall meet in their respective States, and vote by Ballot for two Persons, of whom one at least shall not be an Inhabitant of the same State with themselves. And they shall make a List of all the Persons voted for, and of the Number of Votes for each; which List they shall sign and certify, and transmit sealed to the Seat of the Government of the United States, directed to the President of the Senate. The President of the Senate shall, in the Presence of the Senate and House of Representatives, open all the Certificates, and the Votes shall then be counted. The Person having the greatest Number of Votes shall be the President, if such Number be a Majority of the whole Number of Electors appointed; and if there be more than one who have such Majority, and have an equal Number of Votes, then the House of Representatives shall immediately chuse by Ballot one of them for President; and if no Person have a Majority, then from the five highest on the List the said House shall in like Manner chuse the President. But in chusing the President, the Votes shall be taken by States, the Representation from each State having one Vote; a quorum for this Purpose shall consist of a Member or Members from two thirds of the States, and a Majority of all the States shall be necessary to a Choice. In every Case, after the Choice of the President, the Person having the greatest Number of Votes of the Electors shall be the Vice President. But if there should remain two or more who have equal Votes, the Senate shall chuse from them by Ballot the Vice President.

The Congress may determine the Time of chusing the Electors, and the Day on which they shall give their Votes; which Day shall be the same throughout the United States.
No Person except a natural born Citizen, or a Citizen of the United States, at the time of the Adoption of this Constitution, shall be eligible to the Office of President; neither shall any Person be eligible to that Office who shall not have attained to the Age of thirty five Years, and been fourteen Years a Resident within the United States.

In Case of the Removal of the President from Office, or of his Death, Resignation, or Inability to discharge the Powers and Duties of the said Office, the Same shall devolve on the Vice President, and the Congress may by Law provide for the Case of Removal, Death, Resignation or Inability, both of the President and Vice President, declaring what Officer shall then act as President, and such Officer shall act accordingly, until the Disability be removed, or a President shall be elected.

The President shall, at stated Times, receive for his Services, a Compensation, which shall neither be increased nor diminished during the Period for which he shall have been elected, and he shall not receive within that Period any other Emolument from the United States, or any of them.

Before he enter on the Execution of his Office, he shall take the following Oath or Affirmation:—"I do solemnly swear (or affirm) that I will faithfully execute the

Office of President of the United States, and will to the best of my Ability, preserve, protect and defend the Constitution of the United States."

Section. 2. The President shall be Commander in Chief of the Army and Navy of the United States, and of the Militia of the several States, when called into the actual Service of the United States; he may require the Opinion, in writing, of the principal Officer in each of the executive Departments, upon any Subject relating to the Duties of their respective Offices, and he shall have Power to grant Reprieves and Pardons for Offences against the United States, except in Cases of Impeachment.

He shall have Power, by and with the Advice and Consent of the Senate, to make Treaties, provided two thirds of the Senators present concur; and he shall nominate, and by and with the Advice and Consent of the Senate, shall appoint Ambassadors, other public Ministers and Consuls, Judges of the supreme Court, and all other Officers of the United States, whose Appointments are not herein otherwise provided for, and which shall be established by Law: but the Congress may by Law vest the Appointment of such inferior Officers, as they think proper, in the President alone, in the Courts of Law, or in the Heads of Departments.

The President shall have Power to fill up all Vacancies that may happen during the Recess of the Senate, by granting Commissions which shall expire at the End of their next Session.

Section. 3. He shall from time to time give to the Congress Information of the State of the Union, and recommend to their Consideration such Measures as he shall judge necessary and expedient; he may, on extraordinary Occasions, convene both Houses, or either of them, and in Case of Disagreement between them, with Respect to the Time of Adjournment, he may adjourn them to such Time as he shall think proper; he shall receive Ambassadors and other public Ministers; he shall take Care that the Laws be faithfully executed, and shall Commission all the Officers of the United States.

Section. 4. The President, Vice President and all civil Officers of the United States, shall be removed from Office on Impeachment for, and Conviction of, Treason, Bribery, or other high Crimes and Misdemeanors.

Article. III.

Section. 1. The judicial Power of the United States shall be vested in one supreme Court, and in such inferior Courts as the Congress may from time to time ordain and establish. The Judges, both of the supreme and inferior Courts, shall hold their Offices during good Behaviour, and shall, at stated Times, receive for their Services a Compensation, which shall not be diminished during their Continuance in Office.

Section. 2. The judicial Power shall extend to all Cases, in Law and Equity, arising under this Constitution, the Laws of the United States, and Treaties made, or which shall be made, under their Authority;—to all Cases affecting Ambassadors, other public Ministers and Consuls;—to all Cases of admiralty and maritime Jurisdiction;—to Controversies to which the United States shall be a Party;—to Controversies between two or more States;—between a State and Citizens of another State;—between Citizens of different States;—between Citizens of the same State claiming Lands under Grants of different States, and between a State, or the Citizens thereof, and foreign States, Citizens or Subjects.

In all Cases affecting Ambassadors, other public Ministers and Consuls, and those in which a State shall be Party, the supreme Court shall have original Jurisdiction. In all the other Cases before mentioned, the supreme Court shall have appellate Jurisdiction, both as to Law and Fact, with such Exceptions, and under such Regulations as the Congress shall make.

The Trial of all Crimes, except in Cases of Impeachment, shall be by Jury; and such Trial shall be held in the State where the said Crimes shall have been committed; but when not committed within any State, the Trial shall be at such Place or Places as the Congress may by Law have directed.

Section. 3. Treason against the United States shall consist only in levying War against them, or in adhering to their Enemies, giving them Aid and Comfort. No Person shall be convicted of Treason unless on the Testimony of two Witnesses to the same overt Act, or on Confession in open Court.

The Congress shall have Power to declare the Punishment of Treason, but no Attainder of Treason shall work Corruption of Blood, or Forfeiture except during the Life of the Person attainted.

Article. IV.

Section. 1. Full Faith and Credit shall be given in each State to the public Acts, Records, and judicial Proceedings of every other State. And the Congress may by general Laws prescribe the Manner in which such Acts, Records and Proceedings shall be proved, and the Effect thereof.

Section. 2. The Citizens of each State shall be entitled to all Privileges and Immunities of Citizens in the several States.
A Person charged in any State with Treason, Felony, or other Crime, who shall flee from Justice, and be found in another State, shall on Demand of the executive Authority of the State from which he fled, be delivered up, to be removed to the State having Jurisdiction of the Crime.

No Person held to Service or Labour in one State, under the Laws thereof, escaping into another, shall, in Consequence of any Law or Regulation therein, be discharged from such Service or Labour, but shall be delivered up on Claim of the Party to whom such Service or Labour may be due.

Section. 3. New States may be admitted by the Congress into this Union; but no new State shall be formed or erected within the Jurisdiction of any other State; nor any State be formed by the Junction of two or more States, or Parts of States, without the Consent of the Legislatures of the States concerned as well as of the Congress.

The Congress shall have Power to dispose of and make all needful Rules and Regulations respecting the Territory or other Property belonging to the United States; and nothing in this Constitution shall be so construed as to Prejudice any Claims of the United States, or of any particular State.

Section. 4. The United States shall guarantee to every State in this Union a Republican Form of Government, and shall protect each of them against Invasion; and on Application of the Legislature, or of the Executive (when the Legislature cannot be convened), against domestic Violence.

Article. V.

The Congress, whenever two thirds of both Houses shall deem it necessary, shall propose Amendments to this Constitution, or, on the Application of the Legislatures of two thirds of the several States, shall call a Convention for proposing Amendments, which, in either Case, shall be valid to all Intents and Purposes, as Part of this Constitution, when ratified by the Legislatures of three fourths of the several States, or by Conventions in three fourths thereof, as the one or the other Mode of Ratification may be proposed by the Congress; Provided that no Amendment which may be made prior to the Year One thousand eight hundred and eight shall in any Manner affect the first and fourth Clauses in the Ninth Section of the first Article; and that no State, without its Consent, shall be deprived of its equal Suffrage in the Senate.

Article. VI.

All Debts contracted and Engagements entered into, before the Adoption of this Constitution, shall be as valid against the United States under this Constitution, as under the Confederation.

This Constitution, and the Laws of the United States which shall be made in Pursuance thereof; and all Treaties made, or which shall be made, under the Authority of the United States, shall be the supreme Law of the Land; and the Judges in every State shall be bound thereby, any Thing in the Constitution or Laws of any State to the Contrary notwithstanding.

The Senators and Representatives before mentioned, and the Members of the several State Legislatures, and all executive and judicial Officers, both of the United States and of the several States, shall be bound by Oath or Affirmation, to support this Constitution; but no religious Test shall ever be required as a Qualification to any Office or public Trust under the United States.

Article. VII.

The Ratification of the Conventions of nine States, shall be sufficient for the Establishment of this Constitution between the States so ratifying the Same.
The Word, "the," being interlined between the seventh and eighth Lines of the first Page, The Word "Thirty" being partly written on an Erazure in the fifteenth Line of the first Page, The Words "is tried" being interlined between the thirty second and thirty third Lines of the first Page and the Word "the" being interlined between the forty third and forty fourth Lines of the second Page.
Attest William Jackson
Secretary

done in Convention by the Unanimous Consent of the States present the Seventeenth Day of September in the Year of our Lord one thousand seven hundred and Eighty seven and of the Independence of the United States of America the Twelfth In witness whereof We have hereunto subscribed our Names,
Go. WASHINGTON—Presidt.
and deputy from Virginia
New Hampshire {
JOHN LANGDON
NICHOLAS GILMAN
Massachusetts {
NATHANIEL GORHAM
RUFUS KING
Connecticut {
WM. SAML. JOHNSON
ROGER SHERMAN
New York....
ALEXANDER HAMILTON
New Jersey {
WIL: LIVINGSTON
DAVID BREARLEY.
WM. PATERSON.
JONA: DAYTON
Pennsylvania {
B FRANKLIN
THOMAS MIFFLIN
ROBT MORRIS
GEO. CLYMER
THOS. FITZ SIMONS
JARED INGERSOLL
JAMES WILSON
GOUV MORRIS
Delaware {
GEO: READ
GUNNING BEDFORD jun
JOHN DICKINSON
RICHARD BASSETT
JACO: BROOM
Maryland {

JAMES MCHENRY
DAN OF ST THOS. JENIFER
DANL CARROLL
Virginia {
JOHN BLAIR
JAMES MADISON
North Carolina {
WM. BLOUNT
RICHD. DOBBS SPAIGHT
HU WILLIAMSON
South Carolina {
J. RUTLEDGE
CHARLES COTESWORTH PINCKNEY
CHARLES PINCKNEY
PIERCE BUTLER
Georgia {
WILLIAM FEW
ABR BALDWIN

In Convention Monday, September 17th, 1787.
Present
The States of
New Hampshire, Massachusetts, Connecticut, MR. Hamilton from New York,
New Jersey, Pennsylvania, Delaware, Maryland, Virginia, North Carolina, South
Carolina and Georgia.

Resolved,
That the preceeding Constitution be laid before the United States in Congress
assembled, and that it is the Opinion of this Convention, that it should after-
wards be submitted to a Convention of Delegates, chosen in each State by the
People thereof, under the Recommendation of its Legislature, for their Assent
and Ratification; and that each Convention assenting to, and ratifying the Same,
should give Notice thereof to the United States in Congress assembled. Resolved,
That it is the Opinion of this Convention, that as soon as the Conventions of
nine States shall have ratified this Constitution, the United States in Congress
assembled should fix a Day on which Electors should be appointed by the States
which have ratified the same, and a Day on which the Electors should assemble to
vote for the President, and the Time and Place for commencing Proceedings
under this Constitution. That after such Publication the Electors should be

appointed, and the Senators and Representatives elected: That the Electors should meet on the Day fixed for the Election of the President, and should transmit their Votes certified, signed, sealed and directed, as the Constitution requires, to the Secretary of the United States in Congress assembled, that the Senators and Representatives should convene at the Time and Place assigned; that the Senators should appoint a President of the Senate, for the sole purpose of receiving, opening and counting the Votes for President; and, that after he shall be chosen, the Congress, together with the President, should, without Delay, proceed to execute this Constitution.

By the Unanimous Order of the Convention

Go. WASHINGTON—Presidt.
W. JACKSON Secretary.

[Bill of Rights]

The conventions of a number of the States having at the time of their adopting the Constitution, expressed a desire, in order to prevent misconstruction or abuse of its powers, that further declaratory and restrictive clauses should be added.

Article the first [Not Ratified]

After the first enumeration required by the first article of the Constitution, there shall be one Representative for every thirty thousand, until the number shall amount to one hundred, after which the proportion shall be so regulated by Congress, that there shall be not less than one hundred Representatives, nor less than one Representative for every forty thousand persons, until the number of Representatives shall amount to two hundred; after which the proportion shall be so regulated by Congress, that there shall not be less than two hundred Representatives, nor more than one Representative for every fifty thousand persons.

Article the second [Amendment XXVII—Ratified 1992]

No law, varying the compensation for the services of the Senators and Representatives, shall take effect, until an election of Representatives shall have intervened.

Article the third [Amendment I]

Congress shall make no law respecting an establishment of religion, or prohibiting the free exercise thereof; or abridging the freedom of speech, or of the press; or the right of the people peaceably to assemble, and to petition the Government for a redress of grievances.

Article the fourth [Amendment II]

A well regulated Militia, being necessary to the security of a free State, the right of the people to keep and bear Arms, shall not be infringed.

Article the fifth [Amendment III]

No Soldier shall, in time of peace be quartered in any house, without the consent of the Owner, nor in time of war, but in a manner to be prescribed by law.

Article the sixth [Amendment IV]

The right of the people to be secure in their persons, houses, papers, and effects, against unreasonable searches and seizures, shall not be violated, and no Warrants shall issue, but upon probable cause, supported by Oath or affirmation, and particularly describing the place to be searched, and the persons or things to be seized.

Article the seventh [Amendment V]

No person shall be held to answer for a capital, or otherwise infamous crime, unless on a presentment or indictment of a Grand Jury, except in cases arising in the land or naval forces, or in the Militia, when in actual service in time of War or public danger; nor shall any person be subject for the same offence to be twice put in jeopardy of life or limb; nor shall be compelled in any criminal case to be a witness against himself, nor be deprived of life, liberty, or property, without due process of law; nor shall private property be taken for public use, without just compensation.

Article the eighth [Amendment VI]

In all criminal prosecutions, the accused shall enjoy the right to a speedy and public trial, by an impartial jury of the State and district wherein the crime shall have been committed, which district shall have been previously ascertained by law, and to be informed of the nature and cause of the accusation; to be confronted with the witnesses against him; to have compulsory process for obtaining witnesses in his favor, and to have the Assistance of Counsel for his defence.

Article the ninth [Amendment VII]

In Suits at common law, where the value in controversy shall exceed twenty dollars, the right of trial by jury shall be preserved, and no fact tried by a jury, shall be otherwise re-examined in any Court of the United States, than according to the rules of the common law.

Article the tenth [Amendment VIII]

Excessive bail shall not be required, nor excessive fines imposed, nor cruel and unusual punishments inflicted.

Article the eleventh [Amendment IX]

The enumeration in the Constitution, of certain rights, shall not be construed to deny or disparage others retained by the people.

Article the twelfth [Amendment X]

The powers not delegated to the United States by the Constitution, nor prohibited by it to the States, are reserved to the States respectively, or to the people.

[Additional Amendments to the Constitution]

ARTICLES in addition to, and Amendment of, the Constitution of the United States of America, proposed by Congress, and ratified by the Legislatures of the several States, pursuant to the fifth Article of the original Constitution

[Article. XI.]
[Proposed 1794; Ratified 1798]

The Judicial power of the United States shall not be construed to extend to any suit in law or equity, commenced or prosecuted against one of the United States by Citizens of another State, or by Citizens or Subjects of any Foreign State.

[Article. XII.]
[Proposed 1803; Ratified 1804]

The Electors shall meet in their respective states, and vote by ballot for President and Vice-President, one of whom, at least, shall not be an inhabitant of the same state with themselves; they shall name in their ballots the person voted for as President, and in distinct ballots the person voted for as Vice-President, and they shall make distinct lists of all persons voted for as President, and of all persons voted for as Vice-President, and of the number of votes for each, which lists they shall sign and certify, and transmit sealed to the seat of the government of the United States, directed to the President of the Senate;—The President of the Senate shall, in the presence of the Senate and House of Representatives, open all the certificates and the votes shall then be counted;—The person having the greatest number of votes for President, shall be the President, if such number be a majority of the whole number of Electors appointed; and if no person have such majority, then from the persons having the highest numbers not exceeding three on the list of those voted for as President, the House of Representatives shall choose immediately, by ballot, the President. But in choosing the President, the votes shall be taken by states, the representation from each state having one vote; a quorum for this purpose shall consist of a member or members from two-thirds of the states, and a majority of all the states shall be necessary to a choice. And if the House of Representatives shall not choose a President whenever the right of choice shall devolve upon them, before the fourth day of March next following, then the Vice-President shall act as President, as in the case of the death or other constitutional disability of the President.—The person having the greatest number of votes as Vice-President, shall be the Vice-President, if such number be a majority of the whole number of Electors appointed, and if no person have a majority, then from the two highest numbers on the list, the Senate shall choose the Vice-President; a quorum for the purpose shall consist of two-thirds of the whole number of Senators, and a majority of the whole number shall be necessary to a choice. But no person constitutionally ineligible to the office of President shall be eligible to that of Vice-President of the United States.

[Contested Article.]
[Proposed 1810; Probably Ratified 1819]

If any Citizen of the United States shall accept, claim, receive or retain any Title of Nobility or Honour, or shall, without the Consent of Congress, accept and retain any present, Pension, Office or Emolument of any kind whatever, from any Emperor, King, Prince or foreign Power, such Person shall cease to be a Citizen of the United States, and shall be incapable of holding any Office of Trust or Profit under them, or either of them

[Unratified Article.]
[Proposed 1861; Signed by President Lincoln; Unratified]
Article Thirteen.

No amendment shall be made to the Constitution which will authorize or give to Congress the power to abolish or interfere, within any State, with the domestic institutions thereof, including that of persons held to labor or service by the laws of said State.

Article. XIII.
[Proposed 1865; Ratified 1865]

Section. 1. Neither slavery nor involuntary servitude, except as a punishment for crime whereof the party shall have been duly convicted, shall exist within the United States, or any place subject to their jurisdiction.

Section. 2. Congress shall have power to enforce this article by appropriate legislation.

Article. XIV.
[Proposed 1866; Ratified Under Duress 1868]

Section. 1. All persons born or naturalized in the United States, and subject to the jurisdiction thereof, are citizens of the United States and of the State wherein they reside. No State shall make or enforce any law which shall abridge the privileges or immunities of citizens of the United States; nor shall any State deprive any person of life, liberty, or property, without due process of law; nor deny to any person within its jurisdiction the equal protection of the laws.

Section. 2. Representatives shall be apportioned among the several States according to their respective numbers, counting the whole number of persons in each State, excluding Indians not taxed. But when the right to vote at any election for the choice of electors for President and Vice President of the United States, Representatives in Congress, the Executive and Judicial officers of a State, or the members of the Legislature thereof, is denied to any of the male inhabitants of such State, being twenty-one years of age, and citizens of the United States, or in any way abridged, except for participation in rebellion, or other crime, the basis of representation therein shall be reduced in the proportion which the number of such male citizens shall bear to the whole number of male citizens twenty-one years of age in such State.

Section. 3. No person shall be a Senator or Representative in Congress, or elector of President and Vice President, or hold any office, civil or military, under the United States, or under any State, who, having previously taken an oath, as a member of Congress, or as an officer of the United States, or as a member of any State legislature, or as an executive or judicial officer of any State, to support the Constitution of the United States, shall have engaged in insurrection or rebellion against the same, or given aid or comfort to the enemies thereof. But Congress may by a vote of two-thirds of each House, remove such disability.

Section. 4. The validity of the public debt of the United States, authorized by law, including debts incurred for payment of pensions and bounties for services in suppressing insurrection or rebellion, shall not be questioned. But neither the United States nor any State shall assume or pay any debt or obligation incurred in aid of insurrection or rebellion against the United States, or any claim for the loss or emancipation of any slave; but all such debts, obligations and claims shall be held illegal and void.

Section. 5. The Congress shall have power to enforce, by appropriate legislation, the provisions of this article.

Article. XV.
[Proposed 1869; Ratified 1870]

Section. 1. The right of citizens of the United States to vote shall not be denied or abridged by the United States or by any State on account of race, color, or previous condition of servitude.

Section. 2. The Congress shall have power to enforce this article by appropriate legislation.

Article. XVI.
[Proposed 1909; Questionably Ratified 1913]

The Congress shall have power to lay and collect taxes on incomes, from whatever source derived, without apportionment among the several States, and without regard to any census or enumeration.

[Article. XVII.]
[Proposed 1912; Ratified 1913; Possibly Unconstitutional (See Article V, Clause 3 of the Constitution)]

The Senate of the United States shall be composed of two Senators from each State, elected by the people thereof, for six years; and each Senator shall have one vote. The electors in each State shall have the qualifications requisite for electors of the most numerous branch of the State legislatures.

When vacancies happen in the representation of any State in the Senate, the executive authority of such State shall issue writs of election to fill such vacancies: Provided, That the legislature of any State may empower the executive thereof to make temporary appointments until the people fill the vacancies by election as the legislature may direct.

This amendment shall not be so construed as to affect the election or term of any Senator chosen before it becomes valid as part of the Constitution.

Article. [XVIII.]
[Proposed 1917; Ratified 1919; Repealed 1933 (See Amendment XXI, Section 1)]

Section. 1. After one year from the ratification of this article the manufacture, sale, or transportation of intoxicating liquors within, the importation thereof into, or the exportation thereof from the United States and all territory subject to the jurisdiction thereof for beverage purposes is hereby prohibited.

Section. 2. The Congress and the several States shall have concurrent power to enforce this article by appropriate legislation.

Section. 3. This article shall be inoperative unless it shall have been ratified as an amendment to the Constitution by the legislatures of the several States, as provided in the Constitution, within seven years from the date of the submission hereof to the States by the Congress.

Article. [XIX.]
[Proposed 1919; Ratified 1920]

The right of citizens of the United States to vote shall not be denied or abridged by the United States or by any State on account of sex.

Congress shall have power to enforce this article by appropriate legislation.

[Unratified Article.]
[Proposed 1926; Unratified]
Article—

Section. 1. The Congress shall have power to limit, regulate, and prohibit the labor of persons under eighteen years of age.

Section. 2. The power of the several States is unimpaired by this article except that the operation of State laws shall be suspended to the extent necessary to give effect to legislation enacted by the Congress.

Article. [XX.]
[Proposed 1932; Ratified 1933]

Section. 1. The terms of the President and Vice President shall end at noon on the 20th day of January, and the terms of Senators and Representatives at noon on the 3d day of January, of the years in which such terms would have ended if this article had not been ratified; and the terms of their successors shall then begin.

Section. 2. The Congress shall assemble at least once in every year, and such meeting shall begin at noon on the 3d day of January, unless they shall by law appoint a different day.

Section. 3. If, at the time fixed for the beginning of the term of the President, the President elect shall have died, the Vice President elect shall become President. If a President shall not have been chosen before the time fixed for the beginning of his term, or if the President elect shall have failed to qualify, then the Vice President elect shall act as President until a President shall have qualified; and the Congress may by law provide for the case wherein neither a President elect nor a Vice President elect shall have qualified, declaring who shall then act as President, or the manner in which one who is to act shall be selected, and such person shall act accordingly until a President or Vice President shall have qualified.

Section. 4. The Congress may by law provide for the case of the death of any of the persons from whom the House of Representatives may choose a President whenever the right of choice shall have devolved upon them, and for the case of the death of any of the persons from whom the Senate may choose a Vice President whenever the right of choice shall have devolved upon them.

Section. 5. Sections 1 and 2 shall take effect on the 15th day of October following the ratification of this article.

Section. 6. This article shall be inoperative unless it shall have been ratified as an amendment to the Constitution by the legislatures of three-fourths of the several States within seven years from the date of its submission.

Article. [XXI.]
[Proposed 1933; Ratified 1933]

Section. 1. The eighteenth article of amendment to the Constitution of the United States is hereby repealed.

Section. 2. The transportation or importation into any State, Territory, or possession of the United States for delivery or use therein of intoxicating liquors, in violation of the laws thereof, is hereby prohibited.

Section. 3. This article shall be inoperative unless it shall have been ratified as an amendment to the Constitution by conventions in the several States, as provided in the Constitution, within seven years from the date of the submission hereof to the States by the Congress.

Article. [XXII.]
[Proposed 1947; Ratified 1951]

Section. 1. No person shall be elected to the office of the President more than twice, and no person who has held the office of President, or acted as President, for more than two years of a term to which some other person was elected President shall be elected to the office of the President more than once. But this Article shall not apply to any person holding the office of President when this Article was proposed by the Congress, and shall not prevent any person who may be holding the office of President, or acting as President, during the term within which this Article becomes operative from holding the office of President or acting as President during the remainder of such term.

Section. 2. This article shall be inoperative unless it shall have been ratified as an amendment to the Constitution by the legislatures of three-fourths of the several States within seven years from the date of its submission to the States by the Congress.

Article. [XXIII.]
[Proposed 1960; Ratified 1961]

Section. 1. The District constituting the seat of Government of the United States shall appoint in such manner as the Congress may direct:
A number of electors of President and Vice President equal to the whole number of Senators and Representatives in Congress to which the District would be entitled if it were a State, but in no event more than the least populous State; they shall be in addition to those appointed by the States, but they shall be considered, for the purposes of the election of President and Vice President, to be electors appointed by a State; and they shall meet in the District and perform such duties as provided by the twelfth article of amendment.

Section. 2. The Congress shall have power to enforce this article by appropriate legislation.

Article. [XXIV.]
[Proposed 1962; Ratified 1964]

Section. 1. The right of citizens of the United States to vote in any primary or other election for President or Vice President, for electors for President or Vice President, or for Senator or Representative in Congress, shall not be denied or abridged by the United States or any State by reason of failure to pay any poll tax or other tax.

Section. 2. The Congress shall have power to enforce this article by appropriate legislation.

Article. [XXV.]
[Proposed 1965; Ratified 1967]

Section. 1. In case of the removal of the President from office or of his death or resignation, the Vice President shall become President.

Section. 2. Whenever there is a vacancy in the office of the Vice President, the President shall nominate a Vice President who shall take office upon confirmation by a majority vote of both Houses of Congress.

Section. 3. Whenever the President transmits to the President pro tempore of the Senate and the Speaker of the House of Representatives his written declaration that he is unable to discharge the powers and duties of his office, and until he transmits to them a written declaration to the contrary, such powers and duties shall be discharged by the Vice President as Acting President.

Section. 4. Whenever the Vice President and a majority of either the principal officers of the executive departments or of such other body as Congress may by law provide, transmit to the President pro tempore of the Senate and the Speaker of the House of Representatives their written declaration that the President is unable to discharge the powers and duties of his office, the Vice President shall immediately assume the powers and duties of the office as Acting President.
Thereafter, when the President transmits to the President pro tempore of the Senate and the Speaker of the House of Representatives his written declaration that no inability exists, he shall resume the powers and duties of his office unless the Vice President and a majority of either the principal officers of the executive department or of such other body as Congress may by law provide, transmit within four days to the President pro tempore of the Senate and the Speaker of the House of Representatives their written declaration that the President is unable to discharge the powers and duties of his office. Thereupon Congress shall decide the issue, assembling within forty-eight hours for that purpose if not in session. If the Congress, within twenty-one days after receipt of the latter written declaration, or, if Congress is not in session, within twenty-one days after Congress is required to assemble, determines by two-thirds vote of both Houses that the President is unable to discharge the powers and duties of his office, the Vice President shall continue to discharge the same as Acting President; otherwise, the President shall resume the powers and duties of his office.

Article. [XXVI.]
[Proposed 1971; Ratified 1971]

Section. 1. The right of citizens of the United States, who are eighteen years of age or older, to vote shall not be denied or abridged by the United States or by any State on account of age.

Section. 2. The Congress shall have power to enforce this article by appropriate legislation.

[Inoperative Article.]
[Proposed 1972; Expired Unratified 1982]
Article—

Section. 1. Equality of rights under the law shall not be denied or abridged by the United States or by any State on account of sex.

Section. 2. The Congress shall have the power to enforce, by appropriate legislation, the provisions of this article.

Section. 3. This amendment shall take effect two years after the date of ratification.

[Inoperative Article.]
[Proposed 1978; Expired Unratified 1985]
Article—

Section. 1. For purposes of representation in the Congress, election of the President and Vice President, and article V of this Constitution, the District constituting the seat of government of the United States shall be treated as though it were a State.

Section. 2. The exercise of the rights and powers conferred under this article shall be by the people of the District constituting the seat of government, and as shall be provided by the Congress.

Section. 3. The twenty-third article of amendment to the Constitution of the United States is hereby repealed.

Section. 4. This article shall be inoperative, unless it shall have been ratified as an amendment to the Constitution by the legislatures of three-fourths of the several States within seven years from the date of its submission.

Article. [XXVII.]

[Proposed 1789; Ratified 1992; Second of twelve Articles comprising the Bill of Rights]

No law, varying the compensation for the services of the Senators and Representatives, shall take effect, until an election of Representatives shall have intervened.

APPENDIX B

▼

DECLARATION OF INDEPENDENCE

Courtesy of the Constitution Society. Retrieved October 25, 2007, from http://www.constitution.org/.

Declaration of Independence

IN CONGRESS, July 4, 1776.

The unanimous Declaration of the thirteen united States of America,

When in the Course of human events, it becomes necessary for one people to dissolve the political bands which have connected them with another, and to assume among the powers of the earth, the separate and equal station to which the Laws of Nature and of Nature's God entitle them, a decent respect to the opinions of mankind requires that they should declare the causes which impel them to the separation.

We hold these truths to be self-evident, that all men are created equal, that they are endowed by their Creator with certain unalienable Rights, that among these are Life, Liberty and the pursuit of Happiness.—That to secure these rights, Governments are instituted among Men, deriving their just powers from the consent of the governed,—That whenever any Form of Government becomes destructive of these ends, it is the Right of the People to alter or to abolish it, and to institute new Government, laying its foundation on such principles and organizing its powers in such form, as to them shall seem most likely to effect their Safety and Happiness. Prudence, indeed, will dictate that Governments long established should not be changed for light and transient causes; and accordingly all experience hath shewn, that mankind are more disposed to suffer, while evils are sufferable, than to right themselves by abolishing the forms to which they are accustomed. But when a long train of abuses and usurpations, pursuing invariably the same Object evinces a design to reduce them under absolute Despotism, it is their right, it is their duty, to throw off such Government, and to provide new Guards for their future security.—Such has been the patient sufferance of these Colonies; and such is now the necessity which constrains them to alter their former Systems of Government. The history of the present King of Great Britain is a history of repeated injuries and usurpations, all having in direct object the establishment of an absolute Tyranny over these States. To prove this, let Facts be submitted to a candid world.

He has refused his Assent to Laws, the most wholesome and necessary for the public good.

He has forbidden his Governors to pass Laws of immediate and pressing importance, unless suspended in their operation till his Assent should be obtained; and when so suspended, he has utterly neglected to attend to them.

He has refused to pass other Laws for the accommodation of large districts of people, unless those people would relinquish the right of Representation in the Legislature, a right inestimable to them and formidable to tyrants only.

He has called together legislative bodies at places unusual, uncomfortable, and distant from the depository of their public Records, for the sole purpose of fatiguing them into compliance with his measures.

He has dissolved Representative Houses repeatedly, for opposing with manly firmness his invasions on the rights of the people.

He has refused for a long time, after such dissolutions, to cause others to be elected; whereby the Legislative powers, incapable of Annihilation, have returned to the People at large for their exercise; the State remaining in the mean time exposed to all the dangers of invasion from without, and convulsions within.

He has endeavoured to prevent the population of these States; for that purpose obstructing the Laws for Naturalization of Foreigners; refusing to pass others to encourage their migrations hither, and raising the conditions of new Appropriations of Lands.

He has obstructed the Administration of Justice, by refusing his Assent to Laws for establishing Judiciary powers.

He has made Judges dependent on his Will alone, for the tenure of their offices, and the amount and payment of their salaries.

He has erected a multitude of New Offices, and sent hither swarms of Officers to harrass our people, and eat out their substance.

He has kept among us, in times of peace, Standing Armies without the Consent of our legislatures.

He has affected to render the Military independent of and superior to the Civil power.

He has combined with others to subject us to a jurisdiction foreign to our constitution, and unacknowledged by our laws; giving his Assent to their Acts of pretended Legislation:

For Quartering large bodies of armed troops among us:

For protecting them, by a mock Trial, from punishment for any Murders which they should commit on the Inhabitants of these States:

For cutting off our Trade with all parts of the world:

For imposing Taxes on us without our Consent:

For depriving us in many cases, of the benefits of Trial by Jury:

For transporting us beyond Seas to be tried for pretended offences

For abolishing the free System of English Laws in a neighbouring Province, establishing therein an Arbitrary government, and enlarging its Boundaries so as to render it at once an example and fit instrument for introducing the same absolute rule into these Colonies:

For taking away our Charters, abolishing our most valuable Laws, and altering fundamentally the Forms of our Governments:
For suspending our own Legislatures, and declaring themselves invested with power to legislate for us in all cases whatsoever.

He has abdicated Government here, by declaring us out of his Protection and waging War against us.

He has plundered our seas, ravaged our Coasts, burnt our towns, and destroyed the lives of our people.

He is at this time transporting large Armies of foreign Mercenaries to compleat the works of death, desolation and tyranny, already begun with circumstances of Cruelty & perfidy scarcely paralleled in the most barbarous ages, and totally unworthy of the Head of a civilized nation.

He has constrained our fellow Citizens taken Captive on the high Seas to bear Arms against their Country, to become the executioners of their friends and Brethren, or to fall themselves by their Hands.

He has excited domestic insurrections amongst us, and has endeavoured to bring on the inhabitants of our frontiers, the merciless Indian Savages, whose known rule of warfare, is an undistinguished destruction of all ages, sexes and conditions. In every stage of these Oppressions We have Petitioned for Redress in the most humble terms: Our repeated Petitions have been answered only by repeated injury. A Prince whose character is thus marked by every act which may define a Tyrant, is unfit to be the ruler of a free people.

Nor have We been wanting in attentions to our Brittish brethren. We have warned them from time to time of attempts by their legislature to extend an unwarrantable jurisdiction over us. We have reminded them of the circumstances of our emigration and settlement here. We have appealed to their native justice and magnanimity, and we have conjured them by the ties of our common kindred to disavow these usurpations, which, would inevitably interrupt our connections and correspondence. They too have been deaf to the voice of justice and of consanguinity. We must, therefore, acquiesce in the necessity, which denounces our Separation, and hold them, as we hold the rest of mankind, Enemies in War, in Peace Friends.

We, therefore, the Representatives of the united States of America, in General Congress, Assembled, appealing to the Supreme Judge of the world for the rectitude of our intentions, do, in the Name, and by Authority of the good People of these Colonies, solemnly publish and declare, That these United Colonies are, and of Right ought to be Free and Independent States; that they are Absolved from all Allegiance to the British Crown, and that all political connection between them and the State of Great Britain, is and ought to be totally dissolved; and that as Free and Independent States, they have full Power to levy War, conclude Peace, contract Alliances, establish Commerce, and to do all other Acts and Things which Independent States may of right do. And for the support of this Declaration, with a firm reliance on the protection of divine Providence, we mutually pledge to each other our Lives, our Fortunes and our sacred Honor.

[The 56 signatures on the Declaration were arranged in six columns:]

[Column 1]
Georgia:
   Button Gwinnett
   Lyman Hall
   George Walton

[Column 2]
North Carolina:
William Hooper
   Joseph Hewes
   John Penn
South Carolina:
   Edward Rutledge
   Thomas Heyward, Jr.
   Thomas Lynch, Jr.
   Arthur Middleton

[Column 3]
Massachusetts:
   John Hancock

Maryland:
   Samuel Chase
   William Paca
   Thomas Stone
   Charles Carroll of Carrollton
Virginia:
   George Wythe
   Richard Henry Lee
   Thomas Jefferson
   Benjamin Harrison
   Thomas Nelson, Jr.
   Francis Lightfoot Lee
   Carter Braxton

[Column 4]
Pennsylvania:
   Robert Morris
   Benjamin Rush
   Benjamin Franklin
   John Morton
   George Clymer
   James Smith
   George Taylor
   James Wilson
   George Ross
Delaware:
   Caesar Rodney
   George Read
   Thomas McKean

[Column 5]
New York:
   William Floyd
   Philip Livingston
   Francis Lewis
   Lewis Morris
New Jersey:
   Richard Stockton

John Witherspoon
Francis Hopkinson
John Hart
Abraham Clark

[Column 6]
New Hampshire:
  Josiah Bartlett
  William Whipple
Massachusetts:
  Samuel Adams
  John Adams
  Robert Treat Paine
  Elbridge Gerry
Rhode Island:
  Stephen Hopkins
  William Ellery
Connecticut:
  Roger Sherman
  Samuel Huntington
    William Williams
    Oliver Wolcott
    New Hampshire:
  Matthew Thornton

APPENDIX C

▼

10 USC SECTION 654

Retrieved from the U.S. House of Representatives website, November 18, 2007
http://uscode.house.gov/uscode-cgi/fastweb.exe?search.

-CITE-
10 USC Sec. 654   01/02/2006

-EXPCITE-
TITLE 10—ARMED FORCES
Subtitle A—General Military Law
PART II—PERSONNEL
CHAPTER 37—GENERAL SERVICE REQUIREMENTS

-HEAD-
Sec. 654. Policy concerning homosexuality in the armed forces

-STATUTE-
a) Findings.—Congress makes the following findings:

> (1) Section 8 of article I of the Constitution of the United States commits
> exclusively to the Congress the powers to raise and support armies, provide
> and maintain a Navy, and make rules for the government and regulation of
> the land and naval forces.

(2) There is no constitutional right to serve in the armed forces.

(3) Pursuant to the powers conferred by section 8 of article I of the Constitution of the United States, it lies within the discretion of the Congress to establish qualifications for and conditions of service in the armed forces.

(4) The primary purpose of the armed forces is to prepare for and to prevail in combat should the need arise.

(5) The conduct of military operations requires members of the armed forces to make extraordinary sacrifices, including the ultimate sacrifice, in order to provide for the common defense.

(6) Success in combat requires military units that are characterized by high morale, good order and discipline, and unit cohesion.

(7) One of the most critical elements in combat capability is unit cohesion, that is, the bonds of trust among individual service members that make the combat effectiveness of a military unit greater than the sum of the combat effectiveness of the individual unit members.

(8) Military life is fundamentally different from civilian life in that—

> (A) the extraordinary responsibilities of the armed forces, the unique conditions of military service, and the critical role of unit cohesion, require that the military community, while subject to civilian control, exist as a specialized society; and
>
> (B) the military society is characterized by its own laws, rules, customs, and traditions, including numerous restrictions on personal behavior, that would not be acceptable in civilian society.

(9) The standards of conduct for members of the armed forces regulate a member's life for 24 hours each day beginning at the moment the member enters military status and not ending until that person is discharged or otherwise separated from the armed forces.

(10) Those standards of conduct, including the Uniform Code of Military Justice, apply to a member of the armed forces at all times that the member has a military status, whether the member is on base or off base, and whether the member is on duty or off duty.

(11) The pervasive application of the standards of conduct is necessary because members of the armed forces must be ready at all times for worldwide deployment to a combat environment.

(12) The worldwide deployment of United States military forces, the international responsibilities of the United States, and the potential for involvement of the armed forces in actual combat routinely make it necessary for

members of the armed forces involuntarily to accept living conditions and working conditions that are often spartan, primitive, and characterized by forced intimacy with little or no privacy.

(13) The prohibition against homosexual conduct is a longstanding element of military law that continues to be necessary in the unique circumstances of military service.

(14) The armed forces must maintain personnel policies that exclude persons whose presence in the armed forces would create an unacceptable risk to the armed forces' high standards of morale, good order and discipline, and unit cohesion that are the essence of military capability.

(15) The presence in the armed forces of persons who demonstrate a propensity or intent to engage in homosexual acts would create an unacceptable risk to the high standards of morale, good order and discipline, and unit cohesion that are the essence of military capability.

(b) Policy.—A member of the armed forces shall be separated from the armed forces under regulations prescribed by the Secretary of Defense if one or more of the following findings is made and approved in accordance with procedures set forth in such regulations:

(1) That the member has engaged in, attempted to engage in, or solicited another to engage in a homosexual act or acts unless there are further findings, made and approved in accordance with procedures set forth in such regulations, that the member has demonstrated that—

(A) such conduct is a departure from the member's usual and customary behavior;

(B) such conduct, under all the circumstances, is unlikely to recur;

(C) such conduct was not accomplished by use of force, coercion, or intimidation;

(D) under the particular circumstances of the case, the member's continued presence in the armed forces is consistent with the interests of the armed forces in proper discipline, good order, and morale; and

(E) the member does not have a propensity or intent to engage in homosexual acts.

(2) That the member has stated that he or she is a homosexual or bisexual, or words to that effect, unless there is a further finding, made and approved in accordance with procedures set forth in the regulations, that the member has demonstrated that he or she is not a person who engages in, attempts to

engage in, has a propensity to engage in, or intends to engage in homosexual
acts.

(3) That the member has married or attempted to marry a person known to
be of the same biological sex.

(c) Entry Standards and Documents.—

(1) The Secretary of Defense shall ensure that the standards for enlistment
and appointment of members of the armed forces reflect the policies set forth
in subsection (b).

(2) The documents used to effectuate the enlistment or appointment of a
person as a member of the armed forces shall set forth the provisions of subsection (b).

(d) Required Briefings.—The briefings that members of the armed forces receive
upon entry into the armed forces and periodically thereafter under section 937 of
this title (article 137 of the Uniform Code of Military Justice) shall include a
detailed explanation of the applicable laws and regulations governing sexual conduct by members of the armed forces, including the policies prescribed under
subsection (b).

(e) Rule of Construction.—Nothing in subsection (b) shall be construed to
require that a member of the armed forces be processed for separation from the
armed forces when a determination is made in accordance with regulations prescribed by the Secretary of Defense that—

(1) the member engaged in conduct or made statements for the purpose of
avoiding or terminating military service; and

(2) separation of the member would not be in the best interest of the armed
forces.

(f) Definitions.—In this section:

(1) The term "homosexual" means a person, regardless of sex, who engages
in, attempts to engage in, has a propensity to engage in, or intends to engage
in homosexual acts, and includes the terms "gay" and "lesbian".

(2) The term "bisexual" means a person who engages in, attempts to engage
in, has a propensity to engage in, or intends to engage in homosexual and

heterosexual acts.

(3) The term "homosexual act" means—

(A) any bodily contact, actively undertaken or passively permitted, between members of the same sex for the purpose of satisfying sexual desires; and

(B) any bodily contact which a reasonable person would understand to demonstrate a propensity or intent to engage in an act described in subparagraph (A).

-SOURCE-
(Added Pub. L. 103-160, div. A, title V, Sec. 571(a)(1), Nov. 30, 1993, 107 Stat. 1670.)

-REFTEXT-
REFERENCES IN TEXT
The Uniform Code of Military Justice, referred to in subsec. (a)(10), is classified to chapter 47 (Sec. 801 et seq.) of this title.

-MISC1-
IMPLEMENTATION OF SECTION; REGULATIONS; SAVINGS PROVISION; SENSE OF CONGRESS
Section 571(b)-(d) of Pub. L. 103-160 provided that:

"(b) Regulations.—Not later than 90 days after the date of enactment of this Act [Nov. 30, 1993], the Secretary of Defense shall revise Department of Defense regulations, and issue such new regulations as may be necessary, to implement section 654 of title 10, United States Code, as added by subsection (a).

"(c) Savings Provision.—Nothing in this section or section 654 of title 10, United States Code, as added by subsection (a), may be construed to invalidate any inquiry, investigation, administrative action or proceeding, court-martial, or judicial proceeding conducted before the effective date of regulations issued by the Secretary of Defense to implement such section 654.

"(d) Sense of Congress.—It is the sense of Congress that—

"(1) the suspension of questioning concerning homosexuality as part of the processing of individuals for accession into the Armed Forces under the interim policy of January 29, 1993, should be continued, but the

Secretary of Defense may reinstate that questioning with such questions or such revised questions as he considers appropriate if the Secretary determines that it is necessary to do so in order to effectuate the policy set forth in section 654 of title 10, United States Code, as added by subsection (a); and

"(2) the Secretary of Defense should consider issuing guidance governing the circumstances under which members of the Armed Forces questioned about homosexuality for administrative purposes should be afforded warnings similar to the warnings under section 831(b) of title 10, United States Code (article 31(b) of the Uniform Code of Military Justice)."

End Notes

Deployment:

1. Lawrence, T.E. (1917). The 27 Articles of T.E. Lawrence. *The Arab Bulletin, 20 August 1917.* Retrieved October 20, 2007, from http://net.lib.byu.edu/~rdh7/wwi/1917/27arts.html.

2. Management of the Commander's Emergency Response Program In Iraq For Fiscal Year 2006. *Office Of The Special Inspector General For Iraqi Reconstruction, Audit.* Retrieved October 21, 2007, from www.sigir.mil/reports/pdf/audits/07-006.pdf. This citation is from a Yahoo! search which resulted in a published audit by the Office Of The Special Inspector General For Iraqi Reconstruction in which a footnote references the manual.

3. Obviously, Finance would have had to write off the loss in order to balance the books, but the cash was still gone and unrecoverable. That doesn't answer the question of *why* the officer was required to *draw more cash and give it back* to complete the charade of balancing the books. Without an entry for a write-down of the contract price, the books would never balance in this situation—except in the world of government accounting.

4. Schmitt, E. (2003, February 28). Pentagon Contradicts General on Iraq Occupation Force's Size. *The New York Times.* Retrieved October 22, 2007, from http://query.nytimes.com/gst/fullpage.html?res=9F06E2DA133CF93BA15751C0A9659C8B63.

Gays In The Military:

1. 10 USC Sec. 654, Policy concerning homosexuality in the armed forces. *Office of the Law Revision Council, U.S. House of Representatives.*

Retrieved November 18, 2007, from http://uscode.house.gov/ uscode-cgi/fastweb.exe?search. Full text of the statute can be found in the Appendices.

2. Simpson, A. (2007, March 14). Bigotry That Hurts Our Military. *Washington Post.* Retrieved November 19, 2007, from http:// www.washingtonpost.com/wp-dyn/content/article/2007/03/13/ AR2007031301507.html.

3. Zogby Poll: Don't Ask Don't Tell Not Working. (2006, December 18). *Zogby International.* Retrieved Oct. 21, 2007, from http:// www.zogby.com/NEWS/ReadNews.dbm?ID=1222.

4. Military Personnel: Financial Cost and Loss of Critical Skills Due to DOD's Homosexual Conduct Policy Cannot Be Completely Estimated. *United States Government Accountability Office, Report to Congressional Requesters (GAO-05-299).* Retrieved November 19, 2007, from www.gao.gov/cgi-bin/getrpt?GAO-05-299.

5. Shanker, T., & Healy, P. (2007, November 30). A New Push To Roll Back Don't Ask, Don't Tell. *The New York Times.* Retrieved November 30, 2007, from http://www.nytimes.com/2007/11/30/us/30military. html?adxnnl=1&adxnnlx=1197144094-LSmWKpeccsJnDIzCEO5Spg.

6. Press, A. (2007, May 23). U.S. military continues to discharge gay Arab linguists, and Congress members seek hearing. *International Herald Tribune.* Retrieved November 19, 2007, from http://www.iht.com/articles/ ap/2007/05/23/america/NA-GEN-US-Military-Gays.php.

Farmer's Market:

1. *The Environmental Literacy Council—Superfund.* (2005, November 21). Retrieved November 30, 2007, from http://www.enviroliteracy.org/ article.php/329.html.

2. *Rubber stamping violations in the "war on terror": Congress fails human rights.* (n.d.). Retrieved November 30, 2007, from http://www. amnestyusa.org/document.php?lang=e&id=ENGAMR511552006.

3. "Hale, Nathan", *The Columbia Encyclopedia,* 6th ed. New York: Columbia University Press. Retrieved November 30, 2007, from www.bartleby.com/65/.

4. Olbermann, K. (2007, November 5). *Olbermann: On waterboarding and torture—Countdown with Keith Olbermann—MSNBC.com.* Retrieved November 30, 2007, from http://www.msnbc.msn.com/id/21644133/.

Fear:

1. *Terrorism—Definitions from Dictionary.com.* (n.d.). Retrieved Dec. 5, 2007, from http://dictionary.reference.com/browse/terrorism.

2. Constitution for the United States of America, *Constitution Society Home Page.* (n.d.). Retrieved October 25, 2007, from http://www.constitution.org/.

3. *Foreign Terrorist Organizations (FTOs).* (2005, October 11). Retrieved December 5, 2007, from http://www.state.gov/s/ct/rls/fs/37191.htm.

4. *Ex Parte Quirin et al,* 317 U.S. 1 (1942).

5. Glaberson, W. (2007, July 23). Unlikely Adversary Arises To Criticize Detainee Hearings. *The New York Times.* Retrieved Nov. 27, 2007, from http://www.nytimes.com/2007/07/23/us/23gitmo.html.

6. Kessler, G. (2007, August 6). Weapons Given To Iraq Are Missing. *Washington Post.* Retrieved Nov. 25, 2007, from http://www.washingtonpost.com/wp-dyn/content/article/2007/08/05/AR2007080501299.html.

Betrayed:

1. *U.S. Senate.* (n.d.). Retrieved August 12, 2007, from http://www.senate.gov.

2. *U.S. Senate.* (n.d.). Retrieved August 12, 2007, from http://www.senate.gov.

3. *U.S. Senate.* (n.d.). Retrieved August 12, 2007, from http://www.senate.gov.

4. *Leader—Definitions from Dictionary.com.* (n.d.). Retrieved Aug. 12, 2007, from http://dictionary.reference.com/browse/leader.

5. Franklin, B. (n.d.). *Those who would give up Essential Liberty—Wikipedia, the free encyclopedia.* Retrieved December 9, 2007, from http://en.wikipedia.org/wiki/Those_who_would_give_up_Essential_Liberty.

6. Rich, F. (2007, November 11). The Coup at Home. *The New York Times*. Retrieved November 11, 2007, from http://www.nytimes.com/2007/11/11/opinion/11rich.html?_r=1&oref=slogin.

7. H.R. 1955, Violent Radicalization and Homegrown Terrorism Prevention Act of 2007. *110th Congress, 1st Session*. Retrieved December 2, 2007,   from   http://thomas.loc.gov/cgi-bin/query/D?c110:2:./temp/~c110ieqZZE::.

978-0-595-48193-4
0-595-48193-0

www.ingramcontent.com/pod-product-compliance
Lightning Source LLC
Chambersburg PA
CBHW030322290526
45785CB00001B/477